His Love and My Life

Lalitha Ernest Victor

TRILOGY CHRISTIAN PUBLISHERS
TUSTIN, CA

Trilogy Christian Publishers
A Wholly Owned Subsidiary of Trinity Broadcasting Network
2442 Michelle Drive
Tustin, CA 92780

Manufactured in the United States of America

10 9 8 7 6 5 4 3 2 1

Library of Congress Cataloging-in-Publication Data is available.

ISBN 978-1-64773-576-0

ISBN 978-1-64773-577-7 (ebook)

Contents

Dedication

To

My Love,

Jesus Christ, who gave Himself for me. He came to set me free, leaving His heavenly realms high above. He would have come even if I were all alone in this world. It is He who inspired me to write this episode of mine. I always wanted to write down all the love that He showed us by protecting us and prospering us, spiritually as well as physically. But I never thought I would sit down and write it now. I was walking in the backyard when some kind of light dawned on me. I can't explain what it was, and neither can I remember what it was. I determined to write. All glory and honor, praise, and adoration be to Him and Him alone for His great love. Amen.

To

My Hero,

Reverend Dr. Ernest Victor, a staggering personality for being an instrument in leading me to Jesus Christ and teaching me to have a personal relationship with Jesus. He is a great companion and a life partner. Above all, an awesome prayer partner.

To our long-standing friends and family for their prayerful support and encouragement in my missionary journey.

The Rt. Rev. George Clive Handford
The Rt. Rev. Dr. M. Keith Andrews
Rev. Charles Johnson, The Very Rev. Thomas Phillips
Late Agnes Obed and late Boaz Obed
Late Mr. Jaya Prasad Obed
Late Dr. Joyce Shavanthi Raj
Late Mrs. Deloris Grandfield and Mr. Bill Grandfield
Mrs. Pritha Paul and Mr. Steven Paul
Prof. Anne and Lee Whittaker
Mrs. Eunice Scholten, Dr. Dorothy Samuel
Mrs. Lavina Block and Late Mr. Robert James Block
Mrs. Beverly Lupkes
Mrs. Mary Roberts
Rev. Dr. Dev Prasad
Dr. Lebanon David
Late Dr. L. R. Joshi Rev. Dr. Dev Prasad
Mrs. Diane and Mr. Dennis Conrad
Mrs. Snehalatha Jesudas and Mr. Clement Jesudas

Epigraph

Sing to the Lord a new song; for He has
done marvelous things.
—Psalm 98:1 (NIV)

This book is a new song of the marvelous miracles He did in the Sultanate of Oman and the United Arab Emirates. It was birthed in the heart of my wife, Lalitha Victor, in a moment of divine inspiration and revelation. With no backup journal to go by, she was able to remember retrospectively the wonderful deeds that His holy arm had worked over thirty years. This, indeed, is an inspiration of God the Holy Spirit and an affirmation that God would have her record the past as an encouragement for the future generations.

As we ponder over thirty years, we can only join the psalmist in saying, "The Lord has done this and it is marvelous in our eyes" (Ps. 118:23 NIV).

Our prayer is that this book will challenge the future generations of His faithfulness for the praise of His glory. Amen.

—Reverend Dr. Ernest Victor

FOREWORD

Lives and Legacies

Some years ago, on a hot Sunday afternoon in a small church called the Harwood Raw Memorial Church in Chennai (formerly Madras, South India), we discovered the reason for the name of the church. Until then, the congregation of working-class Tamil-speaking Indians didn't know or didn't care to know why their church had this unusual name. A young English couple greeted a few of the congregation members who were remaining after the service was over and inquired whether they knew the grave site of Reverend Harwood Raw. It turned out that the young man was the grandson of Reverend Harwood Raw and he had come on a mission to discover his grandfather's grave with few details he had gotten from his mother.

We did discover the grave site situated a few meters down the road, after some research. The uncared tombstone was washed clean, and the young man and his fiancée took some pictures to take back to their mother in England. It was then that we learned that Reverend Harwood Raw was one of the early missionaries sent to India by the Wesleyan Mission, almost a century ago. He had lived here in Chennai with his family and established this church, which is now a bustling, busy church in the heart of the city. We also sadly discovered that he had died early, when he was around thirty-five years of age, due to cholera. Had it not been for the visit of these young people, we would never have known about his mission or his sacrificial life.

Sadly, this is not the case of Reverend Harwood Raw only. There have been numerous missionaries, priests, and evangelists whose names and lives may be forgotten, but the legacy of their work remains. I wish to recall one such pastor couple who made an impact in the lives of many people during their tenure in the Middle East.

Reverend Dr. Ernest Victor and his wife, Lalitha, took charge of a traditional Anglican church in one of the Gulf countries, comprising of a dormant, quiet congregation. The transformational change this church experienced during his period influenced many lives from children to adults and elders. Traditional routine church services became dynamic, spirit-filled worship encounters. Sermons were not read from prepared scripts with high-sounding words but simple, power-packed messages that reached out to the congregation. People loved coming to a church that was witnessed by the large numbers, making it necessary to conduct two services in a week. Young people's lives were transformed, some of them committing to obey the calling to serve the Lord in their various walks of life. Both our children, who were adolescents when they took charge, blossomed spiritually under their care and are now serving the Lord in their vocations.

Most importantly, a pastoral care initiative for the hundreds of migrant laborers, called the Labor Camp Ministry, was established during his term. The spiritual and social needs of these hardworking, lesser-privileged men and women were attended to by numerous volunteers from the church, and many from different faiths gave their lives to the Lord. This ministry continues to be a source of care and compassion for these laborers.

We need to remember these men and women of God for their calling and commitment. Even if we don't, the legacy they leave behind will not be forgotten.

—Dr. Irene Nirmala Thomas

Preface

God, in His sovereign power, created the sun, the moon, and the stars in the universe. He created animals and birds and human beings too. When He created each one of them, He saw them perfect. His wisdom and power have no comparison. There is no super being than Him. He is beyond the power of all super naturals. He created the earth, and it was just raw with all kinds of trees, plants, bushes, and reeds. Among them were the wild animals, crawling animals, flying birds, and insects. They were just perfect in His eyes. There was beauty in all that He did, though raw from the hands of the Almighty yet beautiful beyond measure, and that was the original nature created by Him, the Almighty, and He saw them all perfect and beautiful in the eyes of the men too.

One such great place was the Holdsworth Memorial Hospital in a small town of South India called Mysore. All around the hospital was a mini forest where snakes crawled, birds squeaked, and monkeys chattered, with plenty of tamarind trees, neem trees, with one berry tree, and to top it all was a mango tree. Snake holes were here and there, where Hindus came to worship the snakes with flowers and colorful powders, burning sandalwood sticks for the fragrance to the god snake, who they believe is God. I can call this a wild desert or a mini forest of 304,920 square feet.

Mary Calvert Holdsworth Memorial Hospital was founded by the Wesleyan Methodists to serve the women and children who were without proper medical care in the poorer outskirts of Mysore City. Missionaries came to serve the cause of the UK in 1906.

I take pride to say that I was born in this great hospital. My mother, a lovely lady, gave birth to me in such a lovely, serene place. My father was given a house to live there. Most probably, He was one of the very few male workers other than one or two male doctors, a few watchmen, and a carpenter. I and my three brothers graduated and were married in the same town and the same house. We lived there for about thirty years. The snakes sometimes crawled into the houses there, but never to our house. My mother always said, in her simple faith, "It is because we are Christians!"

Years went by, and likewise, days moved on too. All the trees were chopped off. There were no more monkeys, birds, snakes, or snake holes. Modern civilization crept in just as the sun rose in the east.

After high school, I came to an encounter with Jesus. My Jesus held me by my lie. I wept and gave my love to Him. Since then, He has been my life. I was moved by His love, which manifested in my life in the form of grace, which forgave my sins and washed me as white as snow.

I desired to serve the Lord and love Him with all my heart, soul, and spirit. His enriched love compelled me to pass on the passion of His life to others who crossed my path in my life. The love of Christ was a compelling external and internal force that influenced my life to carry on the passion of good news to the rest of the world around me. Christ's love and life sacrifice enriched my life in finding the purpose the Lord has for my life. If Christ came to save the sinful and sick and feed the poor, it is to me Christ came and gave His life as a sacrifice. There is no other God besides Him.

God's love is a Trinitarian love, which is also a Unitarian love. This great Calvary love taught us how to relate to one another in love, how to love our enemies, how to forgive others who ill-treat us, and how exactly to relate to our so-called enemies. The Lord's love, the Calvary love, taught us to base our matrimonial love and experience of one another's love based on God's love, for God so loved the world that He gave His only begotten Son. Ernest and I did form a triangular fellowship ever since we came to know each other; though it was a romantic relationship, it was based on Calvary love, resulting in a triangular fellowship of us both and Jesus with us. We prayed together for others and prayed for ourselves, every day, without fail, to date.

My husband, Ernest, and I enjoyed our career life. He was soon promoted as a senior manager and the head of the Department of Transport in Hindustan Aeronautic Ltd., though the Lord's call for full-time ministry was very evident in his life. I was an assistant professor in education.

We moved on to another city in South India after our marriage. Twelve years of our married life were spent in tasting and sharing the Lord's love with the community around us. God used us to exhibit God's love in having a Bible study and a

Sunday school with five classes and five teachers in our house. No church existed there, as we lived on the outskirts of the city. The Bible study started in two different places, one on the east and another on the southwest, which are now two different churches.

God's passionate love helped us to start a school, called Green Pastures, for slum children of a slum community, utilizing my experience of being a successful teacher/educator. The children were given the gospel, and each carried a Bible as they graduated from the school. The government encouraged the project by providing the teachers' salaries and the midday meal to the students.

For the next twenty years of our married lives, in God's providential plan, we left India and moved to the Sultanate of Oman. Oman, officially the Sultanate of Oman, is an Arab country on the southeastern coast of the Arabian Peninsula. The country shares land borders with the United Arab Emirates to the northwest and Saudi Arabia to the west.

Intimate friends of ours felt that God had rolled a red carpet for us to move over to a Muslim Arab country, where His love through us would be exhibited. Both of us moved there as professionals. After six years of my husband's engineering, he was ordained as a pastor. I continued to serve with the Ministry of Education.

Our ministry began. Not knowing how to swim, we swam, and it was just like us being thrown into the water. We needed all kinds of spiritual gifts, for the problems shared were more than fiction. All that we had to do was to recklessly depend on God's mercy, spiritual discernment, and wisdom. However, our intimacy with God became closer and closer, thereby reflecting His love in our lives. What the doctor could not seek out, the pastor had to. Well, the Lord did. Demons were driven. Possessed were set free. God used us to start fifteen house churches on the northeast of Oman and the main church in north of Oman, where the bishop who signed the Nicene Creed in fourth century AD was seated. In the last six years of our twenty years of stay there, we started a school called Bait Namu Al Tafel (House of the New Beginners) for the local kids three to seven years. There were no such schools by the government. Formal education started at the age of seven-plus only.

Children were told about the birth, crucifixion, death, and resurrection of Jesus in Arabic. They listened to it in awe and wonder. The part of the angel in the birth and resurrection of Jesus was ecstasy for them. We traveled the lengths and breadths, mountains and valleys of Oman, prayerfully and metaphorically, sprinkling the blood of Jesus all over, for the salvation of those who inhabited there.

After twenty years of work in the Sultanate of Oman, we moved on to Sharjah for a pastoral work. Sharjah is the third largest and third most populous city in the United Arab Emirates, forming part of the Dubai-Sharjah-Ajman metropolitan area. The emirate of Sharjah borders with Dubai to the south.

The congregation grew in leaps and bounds. The Holy Spirit worked among them. People gave up addictions and used their talents of singing and music to worship the Lord. Eighty-four congregations met in the building, and an annex was built to hold more congregations.

The wonder of God's love for mankind is measureless. The love of Jesus, manifested in us through His shed blood for the forgiveness of our sins, is forever graceful in us. We have no options other than sharing and manifesting His love through our lives for the rest of the world. The life that is worth living is the life that is led by Christ; the greatest love ever seen or felt on earth is only the love of Christ, a sacrificial love seen only on the cross. This greatest love can only be manifested, forever in practical ways in our lives.

The love of God, how rich and pure and how measureless!

And Lord,
You are the one I desire.
Your LOVE for me has set my heart on fire.
And You will always be the only one,
My risen King,
My everything,
And I will worship You for You are
The only one.
(Vineyard Music, USA)

Acknowledgements

It is a proud movement to thank and be grateful in gratitude to Ernest Victor.

The flower jasmine is often seen as a symbol of purity and innocence, so it makes sense that jasmine flowers are often used in weddings and baptismal bouquets. It is also said that the thread that ties up the jasmine goes up to heaven along with the jasmine. I would connect this as a metaphor for Ernest being a jasmine in my life. His encouragement and advice in nurturing me for Christ was and is invaluable. This book, though it begins with my life journey, sails with both of us and inconclusively ends as both of our journey in mission, expressing the love of Jesus is still on.

1. My deep gratitude to my brother Noel Obed and late Mr. Lionel Sundarm for building up the Green Pastures school while I was away from India.
2. To all the house church leaders in Oman for their full cooperation in hosting the Bible studies in their houses and taking up their roll of leaderships in their towns.
3. To the three teen choreographers in Oman, who got the music and the worship moving.

4. To the deacon in Oman for co-laboring with us in the vineyard of Jesus Christ.
5. To the immigrant workers in Oman, who prayed for us all nights and kept us before God's throne.
6. To the three creative sisters in St. Martin's church for planning all the craftwork for the Sunday school and the summer Bible school and helping me out in the Pearl Sunday school curriculum.
7. To the Sunday school teachers of St. Martin's church, whose cooperation to my innovations were highly motivating.
8. To the council members of St. Martin's church for taking care of our well-being and showering their genuine love on us.

My Parents

My father was born in a village called Chamarajanagar. Chamarajanagar is a village in the southern part of Karnataka, South India, named after Chamaraja Wodeyar IX, the king of Mysore, previously known as Harikutara. It is located on the interstate highway linking the neighboring states of Tamil Nadu and Kerala. Their religion was mainly Hinduism.

The family occupation was the cultivation of the mulberry plants. They fed the mulberry leaves for the silkworms, and they weaved silk out of the cocoons. They would put all the ripe cocoons in the boiling-hot water, and with the weaving machine above the hot water, they would weave the silk. After this, they would send the silk for sale.

I am not sure how my father's family and his relatives came to know the Lord. Those days, missionaries from the United Kingdom did take care of the welfare and education of the villagers and their children. All I know is my father was Obed, his mother was Ruth, and his father was Boaz, and they were first-generational Christians!

He also talked about his tough times in the boarding school. The food they gave was miserable and not tasty. Thereby, we never encouraged him to talk to us about his sad and pathetic school days, which we as children hated to hear. I wish I had encouraged him to speak and share out his heart with us, though. We would have then gathered much more information about his life.

Unfortunately, his school career ended as his father died, owing to an unknown disease, while his youngest sister was in his mother's womb. The mulberry plantation did not yield finance as there was nobody to cultivate it. To make both ends meet, my father had to take up any job that came on his way. He had to make a living to take care of and feed his family as the eldest son of the family. His youngest sister had no idea how her dad looked like. My mother always told me my father was like my aunt's dad and also her brother.

Unlike in Western countries, in India, the parents are responsible to get the children educated and get them married with their expenses and allow their children to carry on their lives successfully without any debt. Since my father had to take sole responsibility for his two younger sisters and a younger brother, he had to help them find jobs and get them married, after which he married my beautiful mother.

I am not sure how he found a driver's job in Holdsworth Memorial Hospital in Mysore (South India), away from his village, Chamarajanagar. The hospital needed an x-ray technician—not sure how the administrators of the hospital came to know my father had high brains! He was sent to Bangalore for an x-ray technician's course. Therefore, he had to send my mother, his first son, and his mother to the village while he underwent the technician's course. It so happened my first brother had some stomach bug. The doctor of the village gave a tablet and asked my grandmother to give half the tablet. My grandmother, by her ignorance, negligence, or forgetfulness, gave my baby brother a full tablet instead of half, which had the opposite effect, and my parents lost him forever. He was no more.

My mother, though came from totally a different culture, had a similar, parallel story to that of my father. It is said that her distant family migrated from Portugal and their language is almost nearer to Portuguese. Her mother died while she was still young, and her father remarried her aunt, who was never married. Stepmothers are normally never mothers. She had a life of foodless days, and therefore a cruel childhood. She was never sent to school, saying the girls needed no education.

After her father's death, some missionaries—not sure from where they were and who they were—took my mother and brought her up. Taught her all the necessities of a successful life. As she was a very beautiful lady, my father, who saw her without her knowledge, fell in love with her. He approached the missionaries to get her married to him. Those were the days when they would never see each other till they were married. My father was skinny and bony; my mother had a fair, beautiful complex. She only saw him on their day of marriage!

My father's career in the hospital was a great success. He was able to innovate many things, and he always enhanced innovations. He worked with FRCF from the United Kingdom, and they together manufactured wax box for leprosy patients, carried on insemination, which was not heard of those days, for those who did not have children. They used ice cubes for anesthesia, manufactured first crutches for those who could not walk. Those were the days when none of those existed. He was a hospital maintenance engineer without engineering studies. Neighboring hospitals also called him to fix all the nonfunctioning medical machines.

Since both my parents had a tough childhood, they loved us dearly and did all they could do, to the best of their abilities, to see that we studied well. They clothed us well, provided well for us, fed us well, and saw each of us had a good career. To top it all off, they promptly took us to church, Sunday schools, and grew us in the nurture of the living Lord, Jesus Christ, who lived on earth, lived and died for us, that we may reflect His love to others in our lives.

My parents were a very loving couple. It appeared as if they were made for each other. The entire community knew about that, as they would see them often going for walks. Those days, couples in India would hardly go for walks. My mother was the best cook for my father; saying so, he would invite friends home for dinner.

Their goal was to educate us well and see that we behaved well. As we grew up, we were very sensitive to our mother's emotions; if we were wrong, she would only shed a drop of tear and that would change us drastically. The family was founded on the foundation of the Calvary love of His, and His great love flew through our parents to our lives, among our siblings. *We will all be there together again in the mansion that Jesus has prepared for us.*

Myself

I was the rose among the thorns—that was what my parents thought of me. The simple meaning of the thorn around the rose is also that: the thorns would protect the rose! My mother would always say they had eight children altogether; the first three sons were taken to heaven at a very early age, and the fourth one was my dearest brother, an apple of my mother's eye. The fifth one is me, the only daughter. Next, two below me are my brothers. I was a naughty, super stubborn, overenthusiastic girl. My parents would take a lot of trouble to please me and meet every need of mine, beyond measure.

I would cry a lot if I felt that my mother had not combed my hair in the way it should be combed. I would make her unplait the hair several times; she plaited and redid it again and again. It so happened once that my mother had to go out to her friend who had just delivered a baby. She asked my older brother to comb my hair and send me to school. I did worry my brother in the same way that I worried my mother. He had a plan. He brought a pair of scissors and started cutting my hair, made it shorter and shorter, till it was beautiful to him. He then happily sent me to school. I was also happy because I looked Western!

I just cannot tell you my mother's reaction when she saw me after I came back home from school.

Since my father worked in the hospital, he was always on calls. In case he had told me that he would take me shopping and was not able to keep up his promise, I would create a big racket at home—no comfort would comfort me. Finally, they would cane me and put me out of the house. I was to stay out of the house until I stopped crying.

Those days, some of the widows or unmarried women in the church were given jobs as Bible women. There was a Bible woman called Sathyajeevama, meaning she is "truthful" in her life. One fine day, when she came home on her visit, I called her out, saying, "Sathyajeevama is full of lies." She was wild when she heard it! I ran and climbed up a tree to escape her wrath. In those days, girls never climbed up trees, but I did.

April Fool's Day was an enjoyable day for my mischief. On one such April Fool's Day, I thought of fooling our full-pledged pregnant neighbor who worked in the laboratory of the hospital, in blood work. I told her there was a patient emergency call for her from the hospital. She believed me, and that was no fun at all. She hurriedly went to the hospital emergency room and discovered that it was just an April fooling. She was fuming with fire, and I had no plans to climb up the tree to escape her fuming anger. It was okay for me, for she had killed all my chicken by poisoning them! But since that day, to date, I have never April-fooled anybody. That is no more a fun game for me.

Our teacher in the school was not happy that I sat next to my friend in the class and was always interested in talking to her, not being attentive in the class. The teacher had no other way of correcting us but to make us sit far from one another. Soon I wrote to my friend, on a small bit of paper, saying, "Here afterward we will only talk to each other on a bit of paper." My friend read it and took the paper to throw it onto the wastepaper basket. A student who sat next to the wastepaper basket read out the letter loudly to the teacher and the whole class. My nerves triggered with fear, but the teacher showed great love toward me with a sweet smile on her face.

In the curricular activities of the school, I was zero. All that interested me were co-curricular activities. I went around with other students, selling tickets for the benefit show for the school building construction.

My cousins lived in our house, as there were no schools near the estates where they lived. I was never happy if my mother showed them more love than me. In India, we wear jasmine flowers or roses or any other flower available to decorate our hairstyles. I always created a racket in our house if my cousin got a little more for her hair.

We siblings fought for silly reasons. Three against one, my three brothers against me, or I against my three brothers. Many times, I would end up with tears for I had no sisters to support me. My mother would conclude by saying that she was there for me. At the age of ten, I was very sick with typhoid. My temperature never came down from 106 degrees Fahrenheit. My parents were highly concerned as they had lost their first three children. They were desperate—my mother never left my bedside. The doctors wanted to give me an ice bath in the middle of the night to get the fever down. My mind was sound, and I argued with the doctors; they decided, even with that high fever, I had a sound mind, so they left me in peace. My mother also remembered, that night, she had a vision of Jesus, who told her that I would be well. Since then, I would have some sort of headache and weakness in my legs, which I would experience only when I lie down on the bed.

I loved sports, games, dancing, dramatics, and athletics. I hated algebra, mainly because when the teacher introduced it, she introduced it distastefully. In games, I excelled while playing throw ball (something like netball); I would play one against nine and would win the game. The physical education instructor called me "monkey." In college, I was called "a spotted deer." Not sure why that name was given to me and what it meant. My language pundit called me Prarabda, which could mean "irritable one," maybe because I always irritated him by being too noisy in the class—perhaps I was stimulated to be noisy because he normally slept in class after teaching for fifteen minutes and wore the same suit every day for one full academic year.

With all my extracurricular activities, I was given an impression by my parents, the school staff, and my friends that I excelled in my studies. Not sure why and how I acquired this super character appreciation. I had a big blow when my board exam results came out. I had to repeat six subjects. My parents' dream for my life must have been shattered. I never dreamed in the wildest of dreams that I would fail in my secondary examination. I had to repeat two sets of subjects, six subjects in all. I spent that academic year focusing on my studies.

When I passed the exam, it was only just a pass. We had to get 105 for 300 in the science group, and the art group of three subjects, we had to secure another 105 for 300 to get a pass. Well, I just got 105 and 108 and barely passed my school exam. I never wanted to fail again. I took my studies seriously. I never knew how to study. My mother was not an educated person, and my father was always busy with hospital work. So, neither of them took interest in teaching us how we needed to study. I would read the lessons once or twice, then I expected to remember the content. I slowly worked hard by making notes and jotting down the points.

I can never forget that Providence was always by the side of me. In my chemistry practical examination, the examiner took up a liking for me and told me the answer! I got through the examination.

In my next examination, my examiner was curious to know how I got my name—one sounded like a Hindu name, and the other like the Muslim name. Lalitha Ambujakshi Obed is my maiden name. The first two names are Sanskrit names and the third is connected to Muslim name Obedullah. I would tell them that Obed is biblical. In those days, most of the Christians had English names. He was friendly, and that helped me do my practical exam well.

I had memorized quite a lot of poems for my masters in English literature, by writing all over the walls, behind all the calendars and cupboards, learning them up now and then. But I just forgot them overnight, soon after the exam. For my Viva, I heard about one particular professor, the head of the examiners, who was very fond of Sarojini Naidu's poems. So, I learned only one of her poems. In the Viva, as I expected, the professor asked me if I knew any of Sarojini Nadu's poems. I did say yes. He asked me to recite one of them. *Zuuum,* I went with all big recitation-style "Palanquin Bearers." He gave me full marks, with high appreciation. Passed out in good grade.

Palanquin Bearers
By Sarojini Naidu

Lightly, O lightly we bear her along,
she sways like a flower in the wind of our song;
she skims like a bird on the foam of a stream,
she floats like a laugh from the lips of a dream.
Gaily, O gaily we glide and we sing,
we bear her along like a pearl on a string.
Softly, O softly we bear her along,
she hangs like a star in the dew of our song;
she springs like a beam on the brow of the tide,
she falls like a tear from the eyes of a bride.
Lightly, O lightly we glide and we sing,
we bear her along like a pearl on a string.

Experience with Jesus

Church and church activities meant a lot to all of us in the family. We attended church regularly. The main churches in our town in our younger days were Church of South India and Anglican Churches. After our days, many other denominations came into existence. Those days, CSI churches did not preach on salvation much. Though they stressed on loving Jesus, most sermons were on the parables or miracles of Jesus. I was the best Sunday school student and also the best in all the children's activities. Therefore, I assumed that I knew the Bible well. Since I completed the senior course in the local Sunday school, I moved on to another Sunday school, about three miles away from our home, where the teaching was done in English.

I had to attend the senior class, as per my age. The senior girls' teacher was a doctor (Ernest's older sister). On some Sundays, she had to go to the hospital. On such Sundays, the girls were sent to the senior boys' class, and their teacher was a male teacher (Ernest). When the Sunday school teacher asked us if we were born again, I assumed I was, because I had learned well in the other Sunday school. "Perhaps I did not know the meaning of it." So, I raised my hand. The teacher did not believe me, for he knew I would have no knowledge of it.

So, he went on further, explaining John 3, what it means to be born again. Now I knew I had openly told a lie by putting up my hand, acknowledging I was "born again."

As I walked home, the Holy Spirit convicted me, saying I had sinned by telling a lie. I wept along the way. I prayed for three nights, confessing all my sins, and asked God to come into my life, and I was born again. A gush of the Holy Spirit came into my being. I experienced the peace of God and His love flowing into my being. All shame and sin were gone. Joy and hope flooded my heart. I normally had a headache since I had typhoid, and that vanished. It was a miracle. Since then, the nights had been a precious time for me to worship the Lord, as I always slept late.

My parents and my brothers came to know my acceptable behavioral changes. There was a huge contrast to my behavior and my older brother's behavior. My older brother was a fine boy with a gentle behavior and was very loving to me and remarkably well behaved with my parents. He was the apple of my mother's eyes, and he highly regarded her, would request her with the word *please* if something had to be done for him. And now my parents noticed me becoming good day by day after being born again. No more stubbornness, no more jealousy. I developed love toward my cousins who lived in our house. That was a witness.

My favorite verse was, "Therefore if anyone is in Christ, he is a new creation; old things have passed away; behold, all things have become new" (2 Cor. 5:17 KJV). To look back and see how naughty I was, how I would beat up my three brothers, how I would keep crying if things were not pleasing to me, how irritable I could be at times, and now to think I was a brand-new creation in Christ was a glorious feeling. That joyous flag in my heart, I would fly it high in the sky and let the whole world know that Christ was in residence there. What an amazing feeling to know that our God is a holy God, and though we are sinful, still He loves us. He hates sins, but not us who own sin. One thing God cannot see is our sin through the blood of Jesus Christ. He loves us, but not our sins, for He is a holy God.

> He will turn again, he will have compassion upon us; he will subdue our iniquities, and thou wilt cast all their sins into the depths of the sea. (Mic. 7:19 KJV)

> Come now and let us reason together, saith the LORD: though your sins are as scarlet, they shall be as white as snow; though they are red like crimson, they shall be as wool. (Isa. 1:18 KJV)

These are the two verses said by Scripture even before the arrival of the sacrifice of Jesus. This clearly depicts the attributes of our merciful God the Father, who loved us so much. He sent His only begotten Son so that none of us should perish and should be forgiven to receive eternal life. God the Father thus fulfilled the Old Testament prophecy by Micah approximately 715 to 696 BC, and Isaiah about seven hundred years before the birth of Jesus Christ.

I told my family about being born again. It was easy to win over my younger brother to the Lord, and he accepted Jesus as his Savior, God, and friend. My older brother, who was always kind and well-behaved, could not really understand the concept of sin and redemption. It was a great mercy of God; two days before his passing on to glory on February 2020 by a serious road accident, a friend of mine went to their house and prayed with him, giving the taste of the Lord's love and His redemptive power. He was extremely happy about this. Joy and peace of the Lord had filled him. He gave me the last call, indicating his joy.

Whenever my younger brother and myself spoke to our father, the way he reflected back on it clearly indicated that he must have also known a little bit of it from his boarding school life. In any case, it was a bit too much for my father, for he said frankly that he had to tell lies; if he were to be born again, he couldn't do that. Often, he teased me and my brother, saying we were Salvation Army people.

My mother also did understand what we were talking about, as she might have heard them from the missionaries, and was very silent about it. For her, going to church and seeing us pray was most important. She took a key position in the women's fellowship. Before her death, she passed information to me that she was saved and was going to heaven. After six months of her sleeping in the Lord, my father also slept in the Lord. We saw him calling out "Jesus!" soon after my mother's death. He used to crawl on the bed and worship the Lord while he missed his wife. We knew he would be in heaven along with his wife, our mother.

Soon after this new experience of being a new creation in our Lord Jesus Christ, I went back to my original church and became a Sunday school teacher there. Perhaps I was the first youngest Sunday school teacher. I enjoyed teaching them and also explained to the children that we needed to tell Jesus all the wrong things we did and then to ask Him to forgive us for those wrong things. That was the year when I trained the kids for the nativity play for Christmas. The funniest thing that happened was, none of the children wanted to become Mary, saying Mary would get a baby. Finally, I had to dress up a cute boy like Mary. The senior Sunday school teacher fumed with fire when she heard this—a boy to be Mary?

The Sunday school, which led me to Christ, sent me to a summer institute Bible training program. Two leaders of the program are worth mentioning. One is the director of the institute, and another was the lady professor. The director was very keen to know if all the attendees knew the Lord personally as their Savior. There was one person who was not yielding to the Holy Spirit. We could notice the director was following this person by supplication. They conducted a special service on the night before the departure of all the attendees. From nowhere, the attendee who had not committed himself to the Lord so far came running to the altar, rolled over, cried, and surrendered his life to Jesus. It was a glorious testimony, and the consistent follow-up of the director was highly appreciated and was a great example of winning over a person for Jesus Christ through prayer and supplication.

The professor was a beautiful elderly lady. For some reason, she had picked a liking for me and wanted to meet me. She traveled all the distance from the town where she lived and came to my town to talk to me. The reason she came to see me was to tell me, "You are a beautiful girl. Many people would like to marry you, but you begin to pray from now on, asking God to show whom you should marry." She was an unmarried lady—maybe she was thus aware that one should begin to pray much earlier for a God-fearing spouse. It was too early for me to consider that in prayer, whom I should marry, but that was her burden to tell me so. I thank God for her and for her advice. I did follow her advice at the later stage of my life.

There was another elderly lady who came to the institute as an attendee. She made a comment that I was a beautiful girl and so would not remain with the Lord forever. This broke my heart into pieces. I wept for two days. The reason I write this is to say my Lord is faithful. "Being confident of this very thing, that he which hath begun a good work in you will perform it until the day of Jesus Christ" (Phil. 1:6). In answer to my tears, my faithful God has kept me faithful unto Himself even till today and would do it till the end of my day.

A friend of my mother, a professor in the university, came to know that I knew the Lord and was just returning from summer school Bible institute, and she requested my mother if I would go to her house, lay my hands on her, and pray for her healing. She was a middle-aged lady, and I was a little too young for her age, but she still believed that God would work a miracle through me. My mother, knowing that she had tuberculosis, did not hesitate to send me to her house. As expected, I innocently went to her house and she gave me some oil and told me to apply it on her head. I did so and prayed. I went there for three or four days. Praise God! I did not hear about her sickness afterward. She was regularly going to work.

There was another aunt who was very close to my mother, knew the Lord, and was full of His Spirit. Some evenings I would run to her house to talk about Jesus, share our thoughts, and pray. She was a great spiritual reinforcement for my life. I praise God for her life. Along with the youth group, we would go to yearly exhibition, neighborhood, house-to-house, and distribute the tracts of "Jesus Loves You."

After coming back from Bangarapet, one of the missionaries in our town asked me to translate the Daily Bread to my mother tongue. I am not good at languages, but still, I was happy to do what she wanted to me to do. I went to her house, which was nearby my house, and did a good job of translation. After a month was over, she gave about ten rupees and sent me home. Those days, this was a great delight for me. I would not like to tell you how much this ten rupees would be in dollars. That was my first God-blessed salary!

With a few other friends of mine, we started a Pioneers Club for girls aged twelve years and below in our Sunday school superintendent's house. All these girls were from Hindu families. We taught spray-painting and pot-painting, lots of Christian songs, and Bible stories. Our Sunday school superintendent was so excited by that she also got nice sets of uniforms to these girls. Thereafter, maybe there was some unhappiness sensed by the parents because the girls were learning Christian songs, so the superintendent closed the club.

College days were simpler days, with studies at home and a few sports. I did participate in athletics and broke a record in the long jump. It wasn't a long-distance jump, but for jumpers of those days, it was long. I also got the women's championship shield for athletics for my final year of study in the university and was published in the local newspaper. Again, the fast runner did not take part that year in the athletics because of some death in the family. So, it was my cup! Blessings in disguise!

I had a good set of friends. We had great fun cycling to college and back. While on the uphill ride, I would bend my body toward the handle of the bicycle and sway my body left and right, pressing forward. That was great fun for my friends who rode with me. No boys would rag us; if they did, we would rag them more.

My father always wanted me to be a doctor, maybe because he was working in the hospital. So, I applied for admission several times. Though there were seats available for medical workers' Christian children in a Christian medical college, I was not selected because of my low grades, and it was also felt deeply by the recruiters that my father could not afford to educate me. If he did, he would only have to sell the property.

The only option left for me was to be a teacher. So, I opted to study bachelors of education. After completing that, I went on to study master's in education. How I praise God for this direction of Him! Teacher! I enjoyed every bit of it.

God's Leading

I was now finishing my graduation. This was the time when the words of the professor who came all the way to talk to me to keep praying for the right man in my life rang bells. Issues of a marriage slowly sneaked in. In our Indian culture, the boy's family had to come forward to the girl's family and ask for the girl's hand in marriage to their son. When these things were happening, I had to begin to pray. I had no intention of really getting married. The Sunday school teacher (Ernest) who led me to Christ was about five years older than me. He was attached to my younger brother, who also came to know the Lord after me. My younger brother did tell him that I was getting offers for marriage. So, the Sunday school teacher decided to come to our house and tell me how the Lord led the missionaries to meet their spouses and the ways in which the well-known missionaries met and got married before they went to their mission field. Well, that was it!

Praying for it was the only greatest tool in my hand, so I decided to fast and pray on Sundays, requesting Jesus to help me know what I should be doing about the matter. I prayed for several Sundays. My mother was not happy about this, for I was a skinny and bony girl.

On a fine Saturday evening, I went to attend a meeting of the Union of Evangelical Student of India (UESI), a group meant for college students. As soon as I entered, I was given a flyer that said, "The grass looks greener and the sky looks bluer when two young people get together." This created a sort of curiosity in me, and as a result, I picked up another flyer to read what it might have contained. That flyer said, "He will fulfill the desire of them that fear him" (Ps. 145:19 KJV). A kind of peace came into my being when I read this.

I went home, had dinner, and slept. In my sleep I had a vision of my Sunday school teacher, Ernest, walking forward. I had no brotherly feeling toward him when I saw this vision. The Lord seemed to tell me, "That is how you should treat him, not as a brother, but as a friend." The next day, when I woke up, I recollected my dream. That morning, my Bible meditation was on Job 33:15–16 (KJV), "In a dream, in a vision of the night, when deep sleep falleth upon men, in slumberings upon the bed; then he openeth the ears of men, and sealeth their instruction." The next morning, when I got up, I recollected the verses, then a kind of peace came into my being, which was very deep and strong. I had never experienced this kind of deep peace in the past. Along with it came a deep, unshakable confirmation and overwhelming peace; that was God's will that I should marry my Ernest.

Later on, I realized, long before this happened, when we were taken to a Sunday school picnic, we had to play a game. In that game, two had to run around, holding hands. Accidentally, my partner was Ernest, whose hand I had to hold and run. We ran well. The Sunday school superintendent, an American missionary, made a comment, saying, "You make a good pair of runners."

I have a sister in Christ; she must be ten or more years older than me. She is a doctor and from the same evangelical background and wanted to keep in touch with me to win me over for Christ. When we met, she discovered that I had already knew the Lord. We became great sisters. That way, God met my need of wanting a sister. It so happened, once I was sick and was admitted to the hospital, during that time, my doctor, this sister, was with me. At the same time, Ernest visited me. After he went, she told me, "You may marry each other one day."

So what next? Though I was full of peace and confirmation on the Lord's leading about the future, it was not easy to carry this thought in my mind all along. I was not sure whom to share this thought with. I did not have the boldness to share this with my parents. Could not share with the friends either, for fear of gossip. It was important to maintain my testimony. Indian culture of those days was so different from that of these days. A girl who fell in love once, if failed, could never think of another boy. A good code of conduct of a youthful girl was honorable to the society and the Christian community.

Meanwhile, Ernest was no more in the town that we grew in; he was by now a full-fledged engineer. He left for another state for work. After many months of praying and thinking, I came to a decision: I would share this to him alone. I was only sure that he would not gossip about it, and he might even rebuke me for such thoughts, and that was okay with me.

On hearing Ernest was in town, I went to see him and just narrated the whole story to him, with my eyes closed. On the contrary, he was fully taken up with what he heard. He was praying that God would send a girl to him! Thus, began the beginning of our love story, to date.

As he left the state to get back to another state for work again, he told me to write letters to him. This was another problem for me. What if my parents did not like this? So, I had to ask my dad for permission if I could write to him. When I asked my father, he just said, "If it is for good, you may write to him."

From that state, Ernest moved on to another state for a training period of two years in a State Road Transport Company. He, a doctor, and a friend were able to start Evangelical Intercollegiate Fellowship of College Students. On October 2019, the students and the staff celebrated the fiftieth golden jubilee of its existence. We praise God for their endurance and zeal for carrying on the ministry successfully.

Thus, we went on and on writing letters to each other. First, we would write about our Bible reading, then we would write what God spoke to us; after that, we would write all that we did throughout the day, and then a little bit of romance here and there. He was also writing journals of all that God spoke to him about in his quiet time. He encouraged me to do it, but sad to say, I could never be that disciplined, whereas he maintains his journey of the Lord's communication with him even till today.

Days went by, perhaps a year, and my mother was unhappy about me writing letters to a boy. One fine day, as we were walking on the road, she expressed her fear, saying, "You are writing letters to a boy. What if the man who marries you objected to it?" For what she said, my answer was, "I would marry only Ernest." She was spellbound. Not a word was said.

By then I had left my home state of Mysore to work in another state called Bangalore. And Ernest worked in a state called Madras, south of Bangalore. Whenever we met, we would meet in Mysore, at our house. We always prayed together, to begin with. We never went out together for any kind of fun. Ernest was a spiritual leader and wanted to maintain his testimony and acceptable behavioral pattern, wholly separated unto God, and not be an issue for the talk of the town.

On a beautiful day in February, we were engaged to be married. Reverend Martin from the UK, who was then in charge of the Evangelical Students Union, got us engaged in the presence of the Lord. After three months, wedding bells rang on May 23 in both of our hometown, in the midst of both our parents. Our Sunday school superintendent was extremely happy that we both, her loved ones, were united to serve the Lord together. The grass looks greener, and the sky bluer, when two get together. The grass looked greener and the sky looked bluer when we got married. Beauty lies in the eyes of the beholder.

Miracles of God

We were now a happily married couple. Adjusting to married life could be an overwhelming time. We realized, only the Calvary love of Christ can be a strong foundation for our marriage. A strong foundation of Christ would help us adjust to married life and transition into life as a married couple for a happier and healthier marriage. It was not really easy to understand each other well during the first three years of wedded life, in spite of our intimacy with the Lord and with each other. Certainly, no individuals are the same, and to get integrated into one being with one thought and one understanding would definitely need the Lord's help.

We had a major issue to sort out. We worked in two different places. Three months after our engagement, we were not sure how and where we were going to make a home; therefore, Ernest had asked me to visit the chief mechanical engineer, who was mainly in charge of giving him a transfer to the place where I worked.

After the engagement, Ernest did get a good job with the government. Therefore, he had to move to another state. I had to move to Bangalore for my teaching position. Soon after I returned to my work in Bangalore, I told the principal of the college I worked at that I was engaged to be married. My principal announced in the class that day that I was engaged to be married.

Soon after the class, an elderly Christian lady student of mine, much older than me, came to me, asking for the details of the man I was going to marry. I gave her the details and told her that he was working in another state. She asked me if Ernest needed a transfer to the city where I was working. She also said she knew a manager who worked in the same government concern where Ernest worked, but in the head office, which was situated in the same city where I worked. If I would go with her, she would introduce me to him. And he might just help us out. Though her suggestion was acceptable, I was not very willing to accompany her to go to that gentleman. She insisted that she would take me to him, in spite of me refusing to go with her several times. Finally, I had no option but to go with her.

She took me right onto his house, and to my surprise, it was the same manager that Ernest had asked to see. He was a very simple man, and I never hesitated to tell him about my engagement to be married to the man who worked under his management. All that he said was to get married and go to his office with Ernest. A great relief, joy, and excitement overwhelmed me. We had only to worship and praise the Lord, whom we cherished. Hallelujah! To God be the glory. All things He has done.

After the wedding, we had to move immediately from our hometown to the city where I worked to join my work. Both of us moved there, but we had no house there; I had lived in a lady's hostel before the marriage. We had a cousin who lived in the same city, so we went and pitched our tent there. My cousin's place was far away from my working place.

We would go out looking for a rental house for our living after my work. My cousin's wife was a much-disciplined lady. Wherever we went throughout the day, we had to be there in their house right on time, when the food was served on the table. If not, she would say no food. At the same time, she would not be happy if we had food in a restaurant. In any case, it was fun to run back to their house when the time was nearing eight o'clock.

We also went to see Ernest's chief mechanical engineer, who had asked me to go to his office and see him after our marriage regarding the transfer. We went to his office. He was a man of few words. Just as he said, he spoke only two sentences. He said, "Congratulations on your wedding. Take leave till you get a transfer." That was to the city where I worked. What a great God we have! We found favor in the eyes of the boss of the world. Just as the boss said, Ernest took one month's leave from the office. On the last day of his leave from the office, he got a transfer order to the place where I worked. Isn't our God a great, miracle-working God? All that we had to do was go to the town where Ernest worked to get a release letter and have a farewell party. Perhaps the chief mechanical engineer knew that Ernest was awarded as the best depot manager for the road transport organization of the state of India.

After we came back to the town where Ernest worked, he joined work in the main office in the city where I was working. We did find a rental house to the southeast of the place where

I worked. There were no churches near that area, though. Only mainline churches were there in the city those days, but none near the house where we lived.

Opposite to our house, an elderly lady lived. She was married to a handsome young man much younger than her. She took care of us, knowing well we were a young couple who needed help. We had to show her our wedding snaps to prove to her that we were really a married couple. We went to their house one day. It was all fun and casual visit. Often, I relax a lot with casual, funny talks. One such talk was about Ernest. I just told her casually, "Ernest is good at dancing," and from then on, she would keep asking Ernest to dance. Finally, I confessed, saying, "Ernest is not good at dancing, but he is good at Bible studies." Well, that was the beginning of quenching her thirst for knowing more of the Lord. A *Bible study* in her house was started. A scientist on vibration also helped out in Bible studies.

We had a two-bedroom house with an office room and a huge living room. Since there was no church and a Sunday school in that area, we decided to start a *Sunday school* in our house. We had four classes and four teachers. Two young adult sisters aged between twenty-two and twenty-five attended the Bible study and came to know the Lord. No sooner had they themselves known they were on fire for God than they were the two teachers of this Sunday school. Two other brothers, young adults, who knew the Lord were also the teachers. We praised God for them. They sincerely loved the Lord and were faithful to His call in serving Him.

We would buy some biblical flashcards from the center of vocational Bible school to narrate the Bible stories. We taught them lots of kids' songs. The parents were extremely happy for all that their children could learn when there were no churches around. The parents also attended Bible study, and sometimes they also hosted Bible studies in their houses. One of the Sunday school teachers is now a pastor. We praise God!

We also had a *youth group* in the house for the teenagers. Two boys who came to know the Lord in the group are now pastors, and another one is a professor in a Bible college. Along with our activities near our house, we were actively engaged in the Sunday school and the mission work in an English-speaking Methodist church that was located a bit farther away from our house. There were no Anglican churches nearby. Though the thought of being born again and saved, or even salvation, was alien to the CSI and the Anglican churches then, still we did not want to leave the church. We decided to stay in the church and witness the love of Jesus and His power of redemption through His sacrifice.

Most of our friends who came to know the Lord along with us have their own churches now. We were never interested in denominational rituals; all that we were interested in was in emphasizing, inculcating, and pursuing the grace of Jesus in His redemptive purpose and to help them to be Christ-centered. Training them to discover what God would tell them by discovering and reading the Word of God.

There was a bank manager's wife who sat next to me in a Bible study. She had complained about her ankle pain. I just kept touching her ankle and kept praying for her healing. Never expressed it to the others in the meeting. She was healed. Though this was the miracle of Jesus, I always protected my ego, lest it might be lifted up. Perhaps I should have learned to exercise in submitting the ego to the hands of Jesus.

The *next perfect miracle* that I witnessed was just breathtaking. I love to hear others praying. There was a graduate intercollegiate prayer meeting, and we had a visiting speaker from Singapore for that meeting. While hearing and joining the prayer, all the attendees were making a big noise, saying, "Hallelujah!" Unfortunately, I could not hear anything that the intercessor prayed. I was very frustrated and disappointed with it. The visitor followed me as I left the hall to wear my shoes. The visiting speaker came toward me and said, "I know you are upset that you could not hear the one who was interceding, but don't worry, the Lord would have heard it all." I was amazed and highly appreciated his discernment! What a gift!

Once in three years, Ernest was supposed to be transferred to another city in the state. This meant that we would have to live in different cities in two different houses. All our mission activities would stand still, or I might have to carry it on my own. Which would be next to impossible. We prayed, and Ernest applied for another job in an All-India federal company, but by God's grace, workers were called forth in an advertisement. He attended the interview, and he had enough holidays to wait for the next job. Finally, he did get that job, and soon, at a very young age, he was promoted as a senior manager and the head of the Department of Transport. God used Ernest to start a Bible study on the way back home. He would take the Bible study once a week. Now this Bible study group has become a Methodist church in that area.

My principal recruited her own niece who had the same subject as I had studied. The management was not happy about this. Therefore, my principal arranged for an interview for both of us; she wanted us to face the management so that the management would select the best one among us. She also hoped that the management would definitely select her niece, because all of them belonged to the same community. I did not take this seriously, but Ernest knew there was something fishy about the whole deal.

By God's grace, I had just completed my three years of experience in teaching in a college of education, and then I had master of education and master of English literature, which was also a feather in my cap. Exact government rule was, one should have three years of teaching experience before teaching in a college of education. I exactly had the same, and the other girl did not. Therefore, the management preferred to have me, but not her. My principal was wild about their decision. She told them they were not fair in choosing a Christian girl, forgoing their own community girl. I just had to praise the Lord. His blessings were bestowed on me at the right time. Hallelujah!

I had completed my master's in English literature online. It was not easy to do without the library facility. A good friend of mine was doing the same as a full-time student, and she helped me with her notes, and also, she loved to combine her study with me. That was a great blessing.

My salary was from the government. It was a little bit higher than doctors' and engineers'. It was just too much for a person who just scraped through in the school certificate exam. Too much of a blessing from my sweet Father, Jesus. Even till today, I will sing of the mercies of the Lord forever. I will sing. I will sing of the mercies of the Lord. Whenever the university students talk about their low grades, I will testify to them by talking about my grades, just 105/300 for aggregate in three subjects. God lifted me up. His blessings are great and are new every morning.

There came a rule for the college of education from the government, that they should maintain a profile pattern in the staff. The first head should be the professor, the principal; next to the principal should be two assistant professors/readers in education. The assistant professors should be in the order of seniority, which was as per their joining the institution. The first assistant professor was a gentleman who joined the institution in the morning, and then it was me, who joined the institution the same evening. I was the youngest on the role, and the promotion came onto my lap, though I was not very keen on it. There were four colleges of education in the city. All the teachers were elderly. It was not easy to work among the elderly. They would always think that I was inexperienced and did not know about the subject as much as they did. It was true. I was selected on the basis of my sports certificate. They called me an “iron rod” at the interview, for they thought I would control the students well.

My responsibility in the college was huge. Apart from teaching principles of teaching and methods of teaching English, I had to maintain ten different timetables for ten different schools, for ten groups of teacher trainees, for two semesters. I had to frame timetables for seven teacher educators to go to these ten schools for supervision. Frame timetables for teaching aid lessons for two subjects and timetables for concerned teacher educators for supervision. Two sets of criticism lessons for their two special subjects, for a hundred students, and the timetables for teacher educators to observe these lessons. Frame examination lessons for a hundred students for two different subjects. Timetables for internal and external examiners to grade the practical examinations for two subjects. Different kinds of staff timetable for the teacher educators. Timetables when they did not have to go for supervision, and timetables for teaching while they had to go for supervision. Not a single error was found either by the principal, the students, or the staff while I framed all these timetables. All wisdom and accuracy were given only by my sweet Jesus. Nothing is impossible for those who depend on Him. "I can do all things through Christ, who strengthens me" (Phil. 4:13).

Apart from the above work, I was responsible for all the internal assessments of the students. I had to collect marks or grades from all the teacher educators and compile them. I did it so carefully that our college got the first rank among all the colleges combined, as long as I did that job. All praise and glory are due only to my precious Jesus.

Every year the owners of our rented house would ask us to leave the house, with fear we might settle down there and not leave their house forever, mainly because we both worked in nontransferable jobs. We could not buy a house too. We did save up some money to buy a house, but by the time we had saved some money, the value of the house also would increase year by year. As a result, we could never buy a house.

Our house was just opposite to a rocky mountain, on top of which was a Hindu temple. During festival time, many people came from far and wide to worship their god. Perhaps one fine farmer who came to the temple must have noticed us walking in and out of the house. He came to ask us if we would buy a piece of land that he owned. We were most willing to go buy it, mainly because that was the need of the day. Along with us, three other friends of ours also bought the property.

Moreover, we did not have money to buy the property, as we had gone to Singapore and spent all the money we had saved. That gentleman was very kind to tell us to buy the property and pay the money later. He got it registered to us just as an elderly brother would to his needy younger siblings. What a great love of God shared and expressed through a man who did not have a taste of the love of a redeemer, Jesus! On every first of the month, he would come and sit on the roadside to collect the monthly installment for the property.

We prayed and asked God to help us utilize it, lest the government might take over. It was a fashion among the teacher educators to start schools those days. Mainly to put all they taught in the classroom into practice. So, our decision was to put up a shelter and start a kindergarten class. The area was surrounded by slums; therefore, we wanted to start a school for slum children, and the medium of instruction would be in their mother tongue. The English medium of instruction was mostly desired by the parents, so we also decided to teach English as a subject, but not as a medium of instruction.

We contacted a local builder to build a room with temporary roofing. We asked God to give us a name for the school. It was

Green Pastures. We also had to have a "trust" or a "society" to run the school, registered in the government. We therefore registered a trust called Green Pastures Education Trust. Unfortunately, this builder was not an experienced builder. He cheated us a lot; he mixed more sand instead of cement and built a roof with only a thin beam. It was sagging.

I continued to teach in the same college of education. I was also getting some extra money for being an examiner, which I would transfer to the school's needs. My big concern was the fragile building construction. We had about twelve children to begin with. While I was teaching in the college, if it rained, I would think of the children in Green Pastures and kept looking outside the window, the raindrops triggering my heartbeat and soul. What if the roof fell off? I would wonder. What if something happened to the children? I would be in prison! Fear would overcome the presence of my mind in teaching.

Another main problem I faced was recruiting teachers to teach these kids. Since it was a mission school, we had decided to recruit the teachers who knew the Lord. A friend of mine agreed to teach them. A few days later, her husband was not happy that she should travel a long distance in order to be with the kids. She volunteered to drop out. The next teacher who came in was also a friend of mine who lived near my house. She came for a short while and asked for a better salary, as it was her essential need. I started praying to ask God to meet her needs. It so happened that the Lord met her need by giving her a good job elsewhere! I had to praise God for answering my prayers and for meeting my friend's needs.

We were on crossroads. We could not find teachers who knew the Lord. We were praying for them. I had no choice but to go in for any teacher who came along the way. One such teacher came to take care of the children. The school would start at eight in the morning to twelve noon, as it was just a nursery school. The teacher was told to be in the school, send all the kids safely home, and then leave the school. In spite of that, her boyfriend would come on his bike and pick her up at 11:00 a.m. It was very scary to leave the children out, as there was a huge pond near the school that almost looked like a lake.

The issue of the lake and the undependable teachers, not getting the mission-oriented teachers to take care of the kids, bothered me a lot. I spent many nights without sleep. My pillow would be soaked with tears as I asked Jesus to find solutions. Ernest would say, "If this project does not give you happiness, why do it?" Ernest worked in the management level, covenanted cadre; he was always busy, and he was not able to help me in any way.

An Anglican pastor was posted next to our house. He took the responsibility of running the Sunday school that we had in our house, and also, he started an Anglican church (Church of South India) in the same place. We praise God for all His good work!

On a fine, beautiful evening after work, I was riding home on a bus when a good old friend of mine got into the bus and sat just behind me. After the conversation of renewing our acquaintance, she asked me if I could do something to help her two younger sisters, who were just at home, not doing anything. Her one sister had done a Montessori training program, and the other had just completed her graduation. The two sisters knew the Bible well, as they belonged to the Brethren mission. My joy knew no bounds when I heard this. I immediately gave her the offer of taking the two sisters to work in our school, the Green Pastures School.

They were excellent at teaching. They taught the children Christian songs and Bible stories every day at a said time. We praise God for answered prayer! They also cleaned the children, as the children were from the slums around. The children were taught to keep themselves clean. We introduced "green uniforms." The doctor friend of mine who is my sister in Christ, who I mentioned earlier in this book, came to the school to check the children periodically and advise medical treatment.

Friends came to know in the church that we were running a school for slum children, so they came to us and said that there were funds for such work, so why not make use of it rather than spending our own money? It was a great, welcoming suggestion. We were extremely happy to know that. A fine day of our hope of anticipation for God's blessings arrived. The director of Compassion for India came to visit us. Teachers were all excited; they scribbled "Welcome" in all different colors on the blackboard. The Compassion acceptance of our school as their project was most welcomed and readily acceptable to all of us. *Praise God! Hallelujah!* Our financial need of the school was blown away by strong winds of mercy and love that existed in the organization Compassion, breathed out by the love and compassion of Jesus.

Another friend of our church who worked in EFICOR (Evangelical Fellowship of India Commission on Relief) came to us, saying he could help us get the bore well rigged for water. That was a great relief as there was no proper, clean water for the children for drinking. I had to provide lunch for the workers when they came for drilling the bore well.

The day dawned when they arrived to drill a bore well for the school. I requested the lady who helped us at home to prepare a good lunch. During my lunch break, I came home to carry the food. On the way home, I borrowed a huge lunch carrier from our neighbor. It was about four feet in length and one and a half feet in width. I was riding a moped in those days. I packed up the food in the lunch carrier, keeping it in between my legs, then I rode on my moped to the Green Pastures School.

When I was about to turn onto my left to enter the school building, the lunch carrier gave up and the food was spilled all over the road. To pick it from the ground with all eyes gazing at me on the road was just a shameful thing. Throwing all that food out was another heartbreaking thing. But I did finally supply food for the workers from a nearby restaurant. All the trouble was worth it. At the end of the day, the water gushed out of the bore well. *The giver of the living water from the springs of water gave us pure, sweet drinking water!*

In parallel to all these, the Lord blessed the handiwork of Ernest. He found favor in the eyes of the management. His boss was a great, fun-loving personality. Moreover, he was happy to have Ernest, who was a workaholic, beside him. He perhaps found it difficult to work seriously. So, the management decided to transfer this manager to another department and promote

Ernest to be the senior manager and head of the department. The boss did enjoy this department, but he could not get back unless and until Ernest left the job or retired. Retirement was never an option because Ernest was much younger than him. Therefore, the only option was to see that Ernest took another job elsewhere.

Opportunity struck well for him. He found an advertisement in the Middle East, in the Sultanate of Oman, for a vacancy in the exact position Ernest was in. The ex-boss gave the advertisement to Ernest and encouraged him to apply. He was successful. Ernest did get the job in the Middle East, in the Sultanate of Oman.

We discussed at home, where our friends from the intercollegiate fellowship of India came and prayed for us. One of the leaders said, "The red carpet is rolled for you, and you should walk on it as missionaries." However, there were two other issues we had to sort out. First and foremost was the issue of the Green Pastures School, and secondly, the conclusion was, since we had no children, we could go. Ernest had an uncle who worked in foreign services. He had no children, and he lived in the same town that we lived in. We thought we would ask him that if he agreed to take care of the school, we could go. When we approached him and asked him, he most willingly accepted it. Most probably, he must have felt that we should also have a taste of living abroad, as he had lived abroad for many years.

The school took care of itself by now. Financially, it was well established. Compassion took care of the nutritious diet for the children, as per the instruction of our doctor friend. Egg and milk were given to every child. Gospel was preached. We borrowed some more money from the bank and got five more classrooms and three bathrooms built. After we left India, Mr. Lionel Sundarm, paternal uncle of Ernest, looked after the school, as he promised us. He was instrumental in getting government approval for the school. He was able to do all the required government approvals most successfully because he was a government official himself working in foreign services and knew how to pull strings.

When he grew of age, not able to function well because of the age, he handed it over to my brother, who built up the school till SSLC (high school). May the Lord's blessing be on those who served the needy children and uplifted them to a higher-status in society.

Before we left India for Oman, we faced a lot of problems renting a house to live. The owners would always ask us to vacate the house every year as both of us worked in nontransferable jobs. They would think that we would live in their houses permanently; therefore, they would always ask us to leave their houses, for fear that if we lived longer, the rent controllers would support us and not the owners. Also, we could never buy a house; whenever we saved money to buy a house, the real estate would always go up. Meanwhile, we had to pay a heavy income tax, for our salaries were very high. We were just an average middle-class couple. To give such high tax in spite of several savings was next to impossible, for it was one man's salary. Perhaps leaving the country was the best option for the said hard issues.

One main thing happened to us just before we left the country. A day earlier to Ernest's departure, the management for whom Ernest worked had decided to give a big piece of land to the officers. I recall the workers from that company coming home that night to get a signature from Ernest, declaring he was the owner of a residential land, which was a great miracle!

If Ernest had left India one day earlier, he would not have gotten that residential land. What an amazing Lord we serve!

We never planned to buy the agricultural land; the landlord came to our doorstep to sell it for us. We did not have money to buy it from him, but he advanced it for us. Our Lord saw to it.

We never dreamed we would start a school for slum children; the land was around the slum area. We never thought we would be the source of preaching the gospel for slum children for several years. It was God's plan.

We never thought or dreamed that we would go to a Middle Eastern country as missionaries; God planned it all. It came to us in circles, round-the-clock.

Our problem with the house was also sorted out. It was next to impossible to find a remedy for it. But God did it.

We didn't have to rent a house anymore—we were moving. Wherever we moved, we were provided with a house free, with no rent to pay. Glory to God in the highest! Amen.

All glory and honor and praise be to Him and Him alone. To the one who breathes His breath on us and the one who leads us and guides us through His breath—the Holy Spirit. We move to the Sultanate of Oman.

The Sultanate of Oman

The Sultanate of Oman is a country of natural beauty intermingled with ancient history and legends. It is the oldest independent state in the Arab world. Oman is considered a hidden jewel. It is strategically placed at the mouth of the Gulf at the southeast corner of the Arabian Peninsula.

The government system of Oman is a sultanate, an Arab monarchy. The chief of state and head of government is the sultan. Haitham bin Tariq Al Said succeeded to the throne on the death of his cousin Qaboos Bin Said Al Said in January 2020. He serves also as the prime minister and the head of the defense and finance ministries and is the chairman of the Central Bank. Judges are nominated by the Supreme Judicial Council and appointed by the sultan.

It is a sultanate in the Middle East on the southeastern edge of the Arabian Peninsula bordering the Arabian Sea, the Gulf of Oman, and the Persian Gulf. It is bordered by Saudi Arabia, the United Arab Emirates, and Yemen, and it shares maritime borders with Iran and Pakistan

The natural resources of the sultanate are huge, which draws tourists. Its natural beauty is visible in its mountains, oases, plains, and seas. The mountain is more than three thousand meters above sea level. It is part of the Al Hajar Mountain Range.

Oman's rich cultural history features traditional forts and souks (market place) scattered across the sultanate. Along with year-round sunshine and unsurpassed warmth and hospitality of the local people, it is easy to see why Oman is emerging as a globally competitive tourism destination.

The country is 100 percent Muslim. Most Omanis (about three-quarters of the country) belong to the Ibadi Muslim faith—meaning they are followers of the Abd Allah ibn Ibad—but there are some Shia and Sunni Muslims as well. Oman is the only country in the Muslim world with an Ibadi-majority population (20, 2017 religious demography.) They are the Ibadis, who number less than three million. Only in one country, Oman, do they form a majority. They see the Qur'an as being created by God rather than a manifestation of divinity itself. The government does not keep official statistics on religious affiliation, but three-quarters of Omanis adhere to the Ibadi sect of Islam, while the remaining 25 percent are either Sunni or Shia Muslims. There are small communities of 5 percent ethnically Indian Hindus and Christians that have been naturalized.

Omanis are the nationals of Oman. Omanis have inhabited the territory that is now Oman for thousands of years. In the eighteenth century, an alliance of traders and rulers transformed Muscat (Oman's capital) into the leading port of the Persian Gulf.

Oman is a high-income country that generates 84 percent of its revenue from dwindling oil resources. Hard hit by the global drop in oil prices, Oman joined the World Trade Organization in 2000 and is heavily dependent on its dwindling oil resources, which generate about four-fifths of government revenue. Tourism, shipping, mining, manufacturing, and gas-based industries are key components of the government's diversification strategy.

The Jabal Shams (Sun Mountain) summit is the highest point in the Al Hajar Mountains, rising at an altitude of 3,009 meters above sea level. Ghul, or Wadi Ghul, is an abandoned village located to the northwest of Al Hamra in Oman. The area is referred to as the Omani Grand Canyon or the Grand Canyon of Arabia. It is near Jebel Shams, the highest mountain peak in Oman. Al-Hajar Mountains, the Rocky Mountains or the Stone Mountains in northeastern Oman, and also the eastern United Arab Emirates are the highest mountain ranges in the eastern Arabian Peninsula.

Oman is an arid country; the climate is characterized by hot and dry summers and mild winters, except for the Dhofar region in the south of the country, which is affected by the monsoon. The average annual rainfall is one hundred millimeters per year but reaches three hundred millimeters per year in the mountains in the north. Groundwater is the main water source, representing 92 percent of the total renewable water resources. Agriculture is the major consumer of water (87 percent of renewable water resources), using a total of 1,124

MCM per year. The total cultivated area is 65,013 hectares, of which 41 percent (26,484 hectares) is irrigated by falaj systems, while the rest is irrigated by wells.

In almost every village, town, and city in Oman, you'll find a long deep path of water running through houses, streets, and farms. This is known locally as the falaj and is the sophisticated main irrigation system in the country. Here are the incredible secrets and technical wonders of this amazing feat (Gehad Medhat 2018).

Falaj systems are most commonly found in the foothills and low lands bordering the northern mountains (Hajar Al Gharbī and Hajar Al Sharqī).

It is not known when the first aflāj was constructed in Oman. In legend, the da'ūdī aflāj (King David) was created by the prophet Suleiman bin Da'ūd (King Solomon), who is thought to have lived in the tenth century BC. He is said to have stayed in Oman for ten days and, because the land was so dry, ordered the jinn demons, (could be strong men)) to dig one thousand aflāj (of the qanat type) every day. This explains why the qanat-type aflāj is called "da'ūdī" (Wilkinson 1977). There is archaeological evidence that the earliest period of falaj construction in Oman dates back to 1000 BC (Al Tikriti 2002), suggesting a pre-Achaemenid origin and consistent with the legend.

Falaj Al Hamra was constructed during the Yac āriba Dynasty by Imam Sultan bin Saif Al Yarubi between 1060 and 1070 Hijri (AD 1,650 to AD 1,660) (Al Shaqsi 1996). Falaj Al Khatmeen near Nizwa was also constructed at this time. Some aflāj (plural for *falaj is aflaj*) have been constructed even more recently, as in the Ibra area, where Falaj Al Yahmady and Falaj Mudhairib are only 150 years old (MRMEWR 2005). Regardless of the uncertain date of the origin of aflāj in Oman, it appears that these systems have provided communities in this area with water for irrigation and domestic purposes for at least 1,500 to 2000 years.

Traditionally, however, the origin of aflāj in Oman has been attributed to Persian influence during Achaemenid times. (Achaemenid was a member of the ruling house of ancient Persia.) It is generally accepted that the technique was used in Persia from at least the end of the eighth century BC. During the midsixth to midfourth centuries BC, it began to be diffused more widely. This was a period of Persian expansion, especially during the reign of Cyrus the Great, and there is abundant evidence from archaeological and historical records of contact between Persia and Arabia (MRMEWR 2006).

Much of Oman came under the Achaemenid rule in the midsixth century BC. And from AD 226, it formed part of the Sassanian Empire of Persia until the Sassanians were finally driven out of Oman with the coming of Islam in the seventh century AD. It is possible that many aflāj were built in Oman in Achaemenid times, and it appears that it was during the Sassanian period that irrigation by aflāj reached its widest extent (Wilkinson 1977, 1983). There was a further period of falaj construction during the Yacāriba Imamates in the second half of the seventeenth century, when the Portuguese were finally expelled from Oman, which became the first independent state in the Arab world.

A falaj gets its water from underground sources, like wells or wadis (valleys). It doesn't use machines to extract water but depends on gravity to force water to flow through its channels. This also controls how water is divided fairly and equally among different farms and surrounding areas. Water is constantly streaming in the aflaj (plural) all year long, but the fullness of the falaj depends on the rainy seasons in Oman, which determine the fullness of the water sources.

The access shafts are built every twenty meters (sixty-six feet) along the tunnel to facilitate ventilation and to help in the removal of debris. There is a ring of burned clay at the shaft mouth, which has two main functions, to prevent the destruction of the falaj if the tunnel collapses and to prevent floodwater from entering the falaj. These covered rings also protect water from pollutants and prevent people and animals from falling in the falaj (Falaj Daris Paolotacchi / WikiCommons).

Three Types of Afalaj in Oman

In Oman, there are three types of falaj: da'ūdī (David), ghailī, and ainī.

The da'ūdī falaj (21 percent of the total number of aflāj) is constructed as an underground tunnel conveying groundwater from the mother well to the irrigated (demand) area.

The ghailī falaj (46 percent of the total number of aflāj) collects water from the base flow of the wadi and transports it in an open channel to the distribution section. During prolonged dry seasons, the discharge of such a falaj decreases and sometimes ceases.

The ainī falaj (33 percent of total aflāj) is fed directly from springs. Many springs that rise from limestone in the mountain areas are reliable sources of good-quality water (International History Seminar on Irrigation and Drainage, Tehran, Iran, May 2–5, 2007, "The Social Importance and Continuity of Falaj Use in Northern Oman," Zaher bin Khalid Al Sulaimani, Tariq Helmi, and Harriet Nash).

History of Christianity in Oman

The inscription shows that the kingdom of Axum (Northern Ethiopia) was in existence in the first century. At the same time, there was a kingdom of the Himarites (a state in Yemen dating from 110 BC) on the Arabian side of the sea; which later came under the rule of the king of Axum. Christianity was introduced into Himayur during apostolic times. Mathew, Thomas, and Bartholomew are mentioned as having a part in it. (Apostles to Islam M world Vol 21 1931 W G. Greenslade)

It is believed in records that the wise men went from the south of the Sultanate, Dhofar to visit baby Jesus. Frankincense was grown only in this place and in Somalia. Persians had then occupied the territory. It is also believed the tomb of Job is in a place called Salalah in the South of Oman. Those days queen Sheba had her moon temple in the south of Oman. The history believes that the queen Sheba ruled five countries those days like; Ethiopia, Egypt, Yemen, Hadramout, and Dhofar. Presently Oman includes Hadramout and Dhofar.

There were the missionaries from the times of the British Navy which was located in Oman. The origin of the Royal Navy of Oman is traceable to the reign of Imam Ghassan bin Abdullah (807–824 AD). He was the first ruler of Oman to possess a Navy, a standing royal navy of Oman was formally established in 1650.

Johann Ludwig Krapf 1810-1881, was a German missionary in East Africa, as well as an explorer, a linguist, and a traveler. Krapf played an important role in exploring East Africa with Johannes Redmann. They were the first Europeans to see Mount Kenya with the help of Kikuyus who dwelled at its slopes and Kilimanjaro (Wikipedia) as he buried his wife and newborn child in East Africa; he believed if the church ever wanted to increase in number, it would be on graves of her members. Truly, the church of Christ in Arabia is a martyr's church.

Thirty-year-old *Henry Martin* landed at Muscat (capital of Oman) on April 20, 1811. He said, "I am in Arabia Felix, with a motto, 'Now let me burn out for God.'" He succeeded in translating the New Testament in Arabic. He was the first modern apostle to Islam.

After Henry Martin, *Bishop French* is considered the second most important Christian missionary to the Middle East, a pioneer missionary. In 1877, on St. Thomas's Day at Westminster Abbey, London, French was appointed the first Anglican bishop of a large new diocese of Lahore, French-reached Muscat, on his final missionary work, on February 8, 1891, and he became the first missionary to visit the region. He had just started setting up his work there when his health started failing, and having been cared for by Portuguese Catholics, he died on May 14, 1891, in Muscat, Oman, and was buried in a Christian cemetery (Wikipedia).

Reverend James Cantine, DD (March 3, 1861–July 1, 1940), was an American missionary, scholar, and traveler. While studying at New Brunswick Theological Seminary in New Jersey, he cofounded the Arabian Mission with John Lansing and Samuel Marinus. The mission exists today as the American Mission Hospital of Bahrain. He was a missionary for forty years, which included establishing the first mission for the Reformed Church in Arabia, which was also the first mission in eastern Arabia. Between 1891 and 1929, he established mission posts, medical clinics, and churches in Arabia. In 1893, Zwemer and Cantine founded in Muscat-Matrah, what was to become *the Arabian Mission of the Reformed Church in America.*

Samuel Zwemer (apostle of Islam), 1867–1952, was born in Michigan. He made his home in Arabia and Egypt for thirty-eight years. He was called by the Arabs "Dhaif Allah," meaning "guest of God." Zwemer lost a beloved brother, Peter Zwemer, and two young daughters to the tropical sun. His amazing comment was, "Simply being dead, our brothers will speak." What hope and what a sacrifice!

Alexander Mackay from Uganda was a Scottish Presbyterian missionary to Uganda known as Mackay of Uganda (October 13, 1849–February 4, 1890). In 1888, two years before his death, he wrote a great missionary document that breathed Christianity in the direction of Muscat as a real remedy for the slave trade. He pleaded to Arabia for Africa's slaves and asked Muscat, which was in more of a sense, to be in stronger Christian mission. "It is almost needless to say that the outlook in Africa will be considerably brightened by the establishment of a mission to the Arabs in Muscat. The Arabs have helped us often and have hindered us likewise; we owe them therefore a double debt. I can see no more effective way of paying them at once establishing a strong mission at their very headquarters—Muscat (Capital of Oman) itself."

Sharon Thomas was born about 1871. Dr. Sharon Thomas died tragically in Oman. He passed away on January 15, 1913. He is buried next to his son in the Christian cemetery, in a cove only accessible by sea. Sharon and his wife, Dr. Marion Wells Thomas, built and ran the first medical clinic in Oman, built in Muttrah, Oman.

Dr. Sharon Thomas was Wells Thomas's father. Dr. Sharon and Dr. Well Thomas were the two generations of medical missionaries for the Dutch Reformed Church in Arabia. When the hospital in Oman opened its doors in 1909, more than ten thousand patients were cared for in the first year, and these numbers never faltered, creating countless lives served and currying gratitude that is still palpable. This fuller history is evident in the careful preservation. Many respondents noted that these good works preceded the economic surge that attended the development of the petroleum industry. Thomas was more than a doctor—he was a hero.

The American hospital in sun-drenched Muttrah was where Dr. Wells Thomas served as a physician for thirty-one years, treating contagious, fatal diseases until his retirement in 1970.

Since then, stories of the noble, selfless man have been passed down through generations of Omanis. Starting with a team of only five Omanis, Well Thomas treated patients in roofless wards under the baking heat, not only in Muttrah, where he lived, but also as far as Barka and Sohar (where we lived, in two houses, in these two different, far-off towns, and functioned our mission work) before roads were built. By the late 1960s, his overcrowded hospital had more than 150 Omani employees, all trained on-the-job. For more than a decade, Thomas was Oman's only doctor, and most of his patients were treated at no charge. Now, forty-six years since the day he left the US, a question arises: Has Oman overlooked the generosity of Dr. Thoms? (*Oman Pride: Book on American Doctor Who Fell in Love with Omanis*, December 5, 2016, 10:13 p.m., Hasan Shaban Al Lawati / hassan@timesofoman.com).

Dr. Donald Taeke Bosch, 1917–2012, was a special surgeon who worked in Oman for most of his medical career and saved many lives. He was a favorite doctor and a bosom friend of His Majesty Sultan Qaboos. The very mention of his name resonates throughout the country of Oman. Dr. Donald Bosch is said to have been a great comfort and help to His Majesty Sultan Qaboos in his ascension to the throne after the death of his father, Said bin Taimur. He was well taken care of by the Sultan, being provided all his necessities and a big beautiful villa on the seashore. We, the Reformed Church missionaries, were invited to his house for a day spent with lavish dinner and friendly fellowship. Dr. Bosh and Mrs. Bosch were a great example to us juniors in their humility and service to the Lord in love and fellowship.

Omanis saw the missionaries' graciousness as sacrificial and inspiration of missionary zeal and enthusiasm. The spirit of care and generosity that drove the missionaries was self-evident in their lives and fully cherished by the local communities. That spirit is still acknowledged, and it transcends other differences between the East and West, between Muslims and Christians ("Legacies of the Mission to Arabia," by Don Luidens, March 1, 2013; he is the son of the missionaries Ruth and Ed Luidens).

The work of *Al Amana Centre* is based on 125 years of collaboration between Christians and Muslims in the Sultanate of Oman. The Reformed Church in America began collaborating with the people in Oman already in the year 1892. In schools and hospitals, they worked together with Omanis to educate and treat people.

In the early 1970s, Oman, along with neighboring countries in the Gulf, experienced rapid development funded by new wealth from *oil revenue.* Since Oman could now fund the hospital itself, His Majesty and the leaders of the Reformed Church in America met to discuss the transfer of the American hospitals in Muscat and Mutrah to the Sultan's new health ministry. In 1973, the transfer was complete, concluding a nearly seventy-year gift of health services from the Reformed Church in America to the people of Oman.

After the closing of the Al Amana School in 1987, the Reformed Church in America established an academic, interfaith center in Muscat as a response to the growing polemic attitudes in the US and Europe toward Islam in general and the Arab world in particular. The purpose was to educate a broad cross section of Christians in the US and Europe about Islam and the Arab culture, with the hope of fostering deeper mutual understanding and peace between the West and the East. Al Amana Centre was established with the approval and blessing of His Majesty Sultan Qaboos, and our work could not be done without our partnership here in the Sultanate of Oman.

Freedom of Religion in Oman

The basic law, following tradition, declares that Islam is the state religion and that Sharia is the source of legislation. It also prohibits discrimination based on religion and provides for the freedom to practice religious rites as long as doing so does not disrupt public order. Christianity is the religion of 6.5 percent of the population of Oman, which equals to about three hundred thousand persons. Ninety Christian congregations exist in the country. There is a little official record of Christianity in Oman until the arrival of the Portuguese in 1504, but ruins from what is thought to have been a church are located in Sohar. Additionally, the Chronicle of Arbela relates the history of Nestorian Christianity.

Almost all Christians in Oman are from other countries. Most of them are from the Philippines, India, or Western countries, and they are concentrated in the country's urban areas: Muscat, Sohar, and Salalah. For many Christians living and working outside of these areas, going to church is inaccessible and therefore only happens on occasion. More than fifty different Christian groups, fellowships, and assemblies are active in the Muscat metropolitan area. The Protestant Church of Oman, the Catholic Diocese of Oman, and the Al Amana Center (interdenominational Christian) are recognized by the Ministry of Endowments and Religious Affairs. There is also a Christian cemetery located in Muscat, operated by the Petroleum development of Oman.

Islam is the official state religion, but Article 28 of the Omani constitution protects freedom of religious practices as long as they do not violate Islamic law. Therefore, Christian migrants in Oman enjoy a considerable amount of religious freedom, although they are bound to strict rules. For example, Christians must practice on specific land that the government has allocated for them. It is also difficult for churches to get permits for construction and permission to host public religious gatherings. Private gatherings are prohibited, although this law is not always strictly enforced.

Proselytizing Muslims is forbidden. There are, however, cases in which a Muslim will adopt the Christian faith, secretly declaring their conversion. In effect, they are practicing Christians, but legally Muslims; thus, the statistics of Omani Christians does not include Muslim converts to Christianity. Instruction in Islam is compulsory in public schools, but there are Christian schools in Oman. A 2015 study estimates a mere 200 believers in Christ from a Muslim background living in the country, and not all of those are necessarily citizens. (From Wikipedia, the free encyclopedia. Religion in Oman)

5.8% of the persons in Oman are Protestant expatriates, approximately 11,500 people. Oman belongs to the area of the Diocese Cyprus and the Episcopal Church in Jerusalem and the Middle East. 21 Protestant denominations are present in Oman and they all fall under the umbrella of the Protestant Church of Oman (PCO). There is a church in Salalah, one in Sohar, and two churches in Muscat. Thus, there are four actual congregations in Oman, all in different languages: Korean, English, Arabic, and Tagalog.

There is a Pentecostal Assembly located in Muscat. Its congregants are largely Indian ex-pats, and it is the largest Malayali congregation in the Middle East. There are over 1,500 members, and service is conducted in four different languages: Hindi, English, Malayalam, and Tamil. (From Wikipedia, the free encyclopedia. Religion in Oman)

The Sultan (King) Qaboos was very favorable to Christians. The visas for the Pastors were sponsored by the king himself through the churches. He loved Hymns and, he would gift organs to churches. Since there were only three main church buildings given by the Sultan for Christians; at the time when we started to work on missions, a church in Sohar was non-existent. The church buildings themselves are located in the coastal cities and are virtually non-existent in the interior of Oman. The three main church buildings located in Oman were 1. Ghala Church 2. Ruwi church 3. Salah church. The church in Sohar was built after a few more years of our work.

When asked us by the Church authorities and the Indian Evangelical Mission; how we would be serving the Lord in Oman. We said, *'we would like to build house churches all over the interior of Oman, the river beds and over the mountainous area; where there were no Churches and those Christians could no way attend the far end churches'*

Therefore, our main passion and the burden was to reach out to the Christian population in the interior of Oman and build house churches all over the interior. With prayer and God's guidance, we moved on to reach out to the towns, on the East coast, the Inlands, and some of the mountainous places.

We had five intimate family friends. All of us knew the Lord. We decided to go to the interior northeast side of Oman every weekend and visit all the Christian friends and have fellowship with them. They were extremely grateful to us, for they did not have any church near them.

God used us (Ernest and Lalitha) to begin our mission in Oman from 1984 to 2004, to get engaged in Bible studies of the church. People were benefited by the Bible studies. Slowly, as the Lord led, we opened house churches by renting small houses all over the northeast and interior towns of Oman. Finally, a church was started by a group of leaders of all denominations at Sohar with a nice big building, where Ernest was the pastor for the Anglican and the Reformed Church of America and was the chairman for all the denominational congregations that met in the Sohar Protestant church.

Mission in the Sultanate of Oman

Ernest, an Engineer

To Such a beautiful scenario, a Muslim country we set our feet on in 1984, with the feathers in our caps of earning a good name and good promotions at a very early age in our career. Now, here we were in a strange country, with no friends around, not knowing what the future held, only knowing that Jesus held our future.

It was a great pleasure to drive there; the traffic rules were excellent. Roads were laid smooth and gray. There were not many parallel roads. One main straight flyover running for about 1,500 km from north to the south. Since there were not many parallel roads, there were not many traffic signals too. There were beautiful roundabouts, each depicting the culture of the country. The Oman National Police were also well-disciplined and were strict in following the discipline of the rules.

They would also say that the bodies of the Omanis were as hard as iron because of the dates they ate. The most nutritious food for them after fasting would be five dates and a glass of water.

In every town of the coastal areas, there were fresh fish markets on the beachside. It was a pleasure to go to the seaside and choose whatever fish we liked. The fishermen were only the Omanis. The fish market had stalls for the sale of the fish, and the Omanis owned each stall, perhaps given to them by the government. They were also good at cleaning the fish. They would clean the fish for a little bit of extra money.

At the airport, we were warmly welcomed by the officers of the company. They had also kept a car ready for Ernest to take off. We were provided with all the facilities, a good, furnished two-bedroom house with no rent to pay. They had loaded the fridge for us to eat and get over the tiredness of the journey. The car was given with petrol, free for any amount of usage. Phone, free. If we had children, their education also would be free.

There were about five managers in the company. All of us lived in one particular area and were good neighbors. The company had one financial controller, a local Omani director, and a general manager. They lived in villas elsewhere. The financial controller was from North India, and the general manager was British.

The financial controller's wife took the leadership role for all the mangers' wives who were from India originally. It was the culture of the company to invite newcomers to their houses for dinner. That helped us to know one another better. Once a year, the managers were given a month's vacation with tickets to go along with their families. Whenever each family went on vacation, it was customary to invite the family for dinner as they went and came back from holidays. About eight to ten dishes were cooked on each of the sendoff and welcome dinners. It was there I learned how to cook. Once a month, the company sent a car with the driver to the wives of the managers to go for vegetable and fruit shopping.

It was not easy to adjust to the new culture, new pattern of life, new acquaintances, new friends, new church, and new ways of thinking and life. Having led a leadership role back in India, I found the situation tough for me to be under the subservient role of the leadership of the financial controller's wife, especially in choices of fruits, vegetables, and the hosting of other officials in the company. It was not difficult for Ernest to get his driving license, but for me, it was quite difficult. Only Omani instructors were allowed to teach driving.

It was good to know a teacher couple from our hometown, Bangalore. Both of them were English teachers. They were slightly younger than us. They were strong believers of the Lord Jesus Christ. We were happy to visit them and were having fellowship with them. They also had a good Bible study group of friends. We were introduced to them, and so it was a great relaxation for us to visit them. There was another Bible study in another friend's house on Mondays. Our friend who introduced us to the group was a great singer and musician. Ernest had to now take the Bible studies, and our friend was in charge of worship and music.

Slowly we began to enjoy all the new fellowships and the friends in the fellowships. They were also like a home away from home. On Fridays, we did have Bible study in the home of another senior couple who worked in the British Petroleum Company. Some staff of the nearby government hospitals also attended the Bible study. There again Ernest was taking Bible study. Often it was combined handling of the Bible study between Ernest and our friend. That was a great combination.

One of our friends, a senior person in the group, was diagnosed with cancer, and it was fourth-stage uterine cancer. All of us got together to pray for her. The Spirit of the Lord asked us to tell her to pray, to ask God to give her life. Only one sentence: "Lord, I want to live." (If she had the desire to live.) That was too simple. We then prayed for the doctors and the nurses who would take care of her. On the surgery day, we waited near the operation theater. Our friend who was a senior nurse was in the theater while the surgery was going on. She came out of the theater crying after a few long hours. She told us it was a serious case, the fourth stage of cancer.

The doctors removed the uterus, a portion of the urinary bladder, and the area all around it. She said the doctor gave her only four months to live. This friend of ours who was undergoing the surgery was a very spiritual, prayerful lady. She had full faith in Jesus that she would live. *Even while the chemo went on, not a single hair of hers fell, and that was her faith. God has given her life even today.*

There was a doctor couple in the main church. The lady doctor was a devoted person, highly spiritual. She enjoyed Ernest's preaching in their church. She would always come and talk to us after listening to the sermon of Ernest. Her favorite worship hymn was, "As the deer pants for the water, so my soul longs for You. You alone are my heart's desire, and I long to worship You." It is from here we heard this song first.

On an early Sunday morning, we heard very bad news that she had fallen asleep in the Lord and she was no more. Our hearts were torn apart. Also, her passion and dream to win souls for the Lord came true on her memorial service. Since she and her husband were well-known doctors in the main government hospital, many top local (Omani) officials were invited, and the sermon was given on that day by a well-known preacher, giving the full meaning of what happened after death to a person who was connected to the grace of the Lord Jesus Christ. *We had to just praise the Lord for what each and every one heard that day. Hallelujah!*

Our life in Oman went on well for eighteen months. I did not know how it was at Ernest's place of work. I only heard from Ernest that on his file there was a "good" remark from his boss, the British general manager. The good remark was mainly because of the work Ernest had done during the peak period of the festival time in Oman.

In parallel to all the good things of the country and the company, we slowly came to an understanding that we were an odd number there. It was tough for Ernest to be a witness for the Lord. All kinds of different lifestyles and fun were there in the company, at the officers' level. Ernest, in their sense of understanding, was most unwanted in the group. On a fine, sunshiny morning, the boss called Ernest to tell him not to go to work in the afternoon. *Ernest came home, wept, and slept. When other officers asked the boss why he did so, he just said, "I don't like to see his face."*

So, what next? Both of us in a foreign land, with no jobs on hand. I had also resigned from my job to join Ernest. It was a shameful thing to get back to India jobless!

This was the end of a story but the beginning of another. We had one month to leave the house. *Where do we go from there?* I wondered.

The managing director of the company was an Omani, a local gentleman. Knowing fully well that Ernest was commended for his good work, which was recorded in the file, he was not happy about what the general manager did to Ernest. He planned to arrange for a job for Ernest in another sister company.

With Christ in the vessel, we can smile at the storm.

"It is of the LORD's mercies that we are not consumed because his compassions fail not. They are new every morning: great is thy faithfulness" (Lam. 3:22–23 KIVA).

What Next?

The Lord held us together. Though emotionally and physically drained, we did not break. The ship of our soul was steady though the storm in the sea was high. We were held together by our Lord, our Savior. Our friends from our church were of great support, spiritually, emotionally, and physically.

During the time of turbulence, the Lord taught us how to pray on serious issues, for we did not know what to pray for and how to pray. We just prayed in general for some prayers on certain complicated issues as we kept on praying that the Lord would guide us to understand the issue as per His wisdom in the given situation, in analyzing and interpreting them and then coming to conclusions. It would be a slow process. The

Holy Spirit would help us to pinpoint the center of His will on the issue that needed prayer. When prayed on, the answer would come. Under normal situations, things prayed for would also be answered spontaneously.

We also believed that whenever we prayed, it is we who prayed, but I believe it is my Master who often initiates my companionship with Him. How often I want to pray but there wouldn't be a deep concentration. Sometimes when I do have a deep concentration in praying, *I do believe then it is only the gift of God. I have sensed this kind of deep concentration, unaware of myself,* when I sit under a tree or at the backyard, or I walk on the road and the Lord calls me to be with Him, enjoying His beauty and holiness in all that I see. Sometimes, when I recognize His Spirit moving in me and calling me to worship Him and intercede, I feel like grabbing that moment and saying all that I want to say to Him. "Ah, here it is, let me have it full" would be the longing, grabbing kind of an intention to be with the Lord.

The sister company willingly wanted to give a position to Ernest. Unfortunately, it was not as per his qualification, but it was just a job, a kind of supervision. The contract for a job in Oman was for two years. If one changed the job in two years, one had to exit the country and make an entry back with a new visa for the new company. Also, then one could buy another car and also a new residential phone in the name of the company. The police could check these requirements anytime, and the severity of the punishment would depend upon the depth of the irregularities.

The new company also promised for another house. We were asked to vacate the present company house within a month. The anxiety and the tension of leaving the house and not being sure of the timings and the date of the availability of the new house were at their peak. But God worked it out well; just one day before our said date, we were given the key to the new house. This house was better than the previous house. It was a villa. God took us to a breaking point but did not allow us to be broken.

All ended up in praising and giving honor and glory to the living Lord Jesus Christ. The house was well furnished, and a good set of crockery and silver spoons was provided. It was in the heart of the carpentry workshop. Though some friends visited us, we could not have a Bible study there. We did have good fellowship and friendship with our friends from the church, and we continued to visit our friends in the rural areas, in the northeast of Oman, to have Bible studies and prayer, as they did not have a church nearby. Neither did they have cars to commute. Most of them were hospital workers.

Meanwhile, we went to the Ministry of Education to look for a job for me. There were no job vacancies for me near Ernest's workplace. So, they gave me a job in another town, with a promise they would transfer me back during the next academic year. It was the law of the country that we should work only with the sponsored companies. In case we worked in a different company that had not sponsored, one had to be sent out of the country or criminal action could be taken against the one who broke the law. My sponsorship was from the company that Ernest worked. Therefore, I now had to enter into another sponsorship, where I would be working. My job was from the Ministry of Education of Oman. Therefore, I had to get my certifications attested by the Ministry of Education in India. This procedure took some considerable time.

We lived in a town called Azaiba in Oman. The work given to me was in Musanna, about fifty-seven miles from our house, in the northeast of Oman. The status quo of the country was such that only the laborers and those who could not afford cars to commute were to travel in cabs. There was no bus service too. It was not safe for the ladies to travel by cabs. Therefore, for me to commute to work from home to the school was a Herculean task. We could not own a car because Ernest was under another sponsorship.

I, having no car of ours, had to go home only during weekends and holidays. My case was one such case where I had to prove my husband worked in Oman, and my marriage ties. This strict arrangement was made especially for the Arab teachers, which in turn meant for all the teachers, without any racial bias. The common rule of Oman was, all the expatriates were given accommodation to live, and the deviation of which was strictly prohibited. There were not many local teachers when I joined work.

Our new house was in Azaiba. I had to commute every day from Azaiba to Musanna, where my school was, for forty-four minutes. The distance between these two places was ninety-two kilometers, fifty-seven miles; as per the job contract, the accommodation was given by the Ministry of Education. For single teachers, accommodation given was single rooms with attached bathrooms; for teachers with family, villas were given. They could rent houses anywhere, but a fixed amount was given to them for rent every month.

I had to commute to school on weekdays and stay in the given accommodation. Some of us lady teachers were given a villa, in which there were six Egyptian teachers. They did not know English, and nor did I know Arabic. All of them lived inside the villa, but I had to stay in a room outside the villa, which had no bathroom. For weekends, I would get back home, where Ernest lived. Our weekends were on Fridays and Saturdays. Fridays were their worship days. *These weekends were very special to us. We clung on to each other as if we had never seen each other for centuries.* As I have said earlier, for obvious reasons, we did not have a car. So, our friends, a couple, would come home right on time to take me to the school and leave me at the place where I lived.

Our friends, along with Ernest, would leave me to school every Friday evening, but they could not bring me back after school on Thursdays at noon, mainly because they had to be at work. I had to travel alone, picking up a cab. Even to go to the main road, I had to stand all by myself in the middle of the desert, waiting for the cab, which passed by the main road. Only the Omani drivers were allowed to drive a cab. It was very fearful to travel with an unknown Omani driver. *To stand in the middle of the desert, with no houses or no passersby, was a fearful thing. Though I felt fear in my bones, still I could face it because my Lord's grace was in abundance.*

The travel was slowly becoming very special to me. The semidesert scenario and the lovely layout of the road leading to a smooth driveway were enjoyable. On the way, there were many nice Indian restaurants to choose from and have our dinner.

For me to leave Ernest all by himself in a strange, new place back at home was a very painful feeling. We never liked to be without the other's company ever since we got married. I began to worry about his loneliness. We faced the possibility of our deep separation with prayer. My Jesus was very close to me at that time. He would speak to me at times of trouble and doubt and increase my faith. *If I am worried about Ernest, I thought, how much would our Jesus, who gave His life for us, worry about Ernest?* He would tenderly watch over him. Therefore, I need not be worried about Ernest. "O Jerusalem, Jerusalem, which kills the prophets, and stones them that are sent unto thee; how often would I have gathered thy children together, as a hen doth gather her brood under her wings, and ye would not" (Luke 13:34 KJV).

My room was outside the villa. A small room. Maybe a room of six by seven feet. I had space to keep a small stool at the corner and a bed in another corner. It had a door, of course, and a window. During the daytime, if I looked outside the window, I would only see a vast desert and dunes. During night times, if I looked outside the window, I would only see beautiful dark-blue stars in the sky, which God created beautifully.

Most of the subject teachers were from Egypt, and some were from Tunisia, because the medium of instruction was in Arabic. English teachers were from other countries. Single teachers without their families were to stay in the accommodation provided by the Ministry of Education. Each school had such accommodation for their teachers. Those who had their families and spouses could live with their families, provided they submitted their wedding certificates and proof to say that they were the genuine spouses! If the teachers did want the school to provide accommodation upon finding it difficult to commute to the school every day from their houses, they could take a school-provided accommodation, and if they wanted to go to their houses for weekends and holidays, they should again need to take official permission from the school accommodation authorities.

On some days, all the Egyptian teachers would be crying loudly. If asked why they were doing so, they would say, "No letters from our husbands. They must have gotten married again." With all said, it was not easy to live with six ladies without their children and husbands in Oman, left behind in Egypt. One came to sit on my bed to talk on certain things, and I was deathly afraid of her. Though I shared everything with Ernest, I kept certain things away from him. Lest he worried. Despite all that, *God protected me inch by inch and millimeter by millimeter. Praise Him! Hallelujah!*

Though my room was very small, it was cozy. I would keep it clean and nicely arranged. On the stool I would keep a small vase and a beautiful flower or a cactus. The beauty of it created a sense of devotion to God, who created it. I would start worshipping the living God, and loneliness would flee. Peace and the joy of the Lord excelled in me.

As I traveled from home to school and back home from school, *I would notice a Muslim Bedouin all alone, spreading a prayer carpet under the tree, bowing down, falling prostrate toward the east, sincerely worshipping his god. Nobody to watch him, with no Pharisee mentality, all by himself, worshipping the god whom he believed in. Many Bedouins did this as they traveled that path. Amazingly, they always carried heavy prayer carpets. What an awesome reverence to God! I wondered if I had this reverence and worship toward my living God.*

On the contrary to the Bedouin, the teachers who taught with me had adopted an entirely different style of worship. They would also have a common prayer carpet. They would pick it up in the staff room, fall prostrate on it while everybody watched their sincerity toward reverence and worship toward their god. During their fasting on Ramadan days, they would keep talking about different kinds of recipes. Now and then they would put the carpet and pray. *First time I experienced in reality what Jesus said regarding the Pharisees.*

While in India, as I grew up, and as an adult, I was of the strongest of opinion that only those who believe in Jesus would go to heaven. Though the dominant three main religions were Hindus, Christianity, and Islam, I am of deep understanding that it is Christianity that is accepted by one and all as the only religion to go to heaven soon after the believer's death, because of the redemptive power of Jesus. *Here I was facing a bunch of teachers who said that one has to become a Muslim to go to heaven and were insistent that I should become a Muslim!*

The religious teacher would also tell the students to talk to me about it. At the beginning of my career, I would just listen to whatever they would say. They would also know that I was a strong Christian by my behavior. I did respect their views on the dressing. They would not appreciate me wearing half-sleeves and a low-neck blouse. They would not like to see the back exposed with lower neckwear. If I did so, that would be sinful, to expose the woman's back. I respected their views and was, in every way, modest in dressing. Praise the Lord! I could not witness in words or preach in the school. Except to witness to them in my behavior, that I was a good Christian and a good teacher, all because of my Jesus, who pruned me so well.

I taught in that school only for about six months. As promised, I was given a school that was nearer to our house. That was only about forty-five miles away from the house. The school also had a good accommodation for me. There were only three of us, and the building was within the school compound. It was a much safer place for ladies.

Since the contract period of the previous company was over, Ernest was now eligible to get another, new contract with the present company and would be considered as a legal resident of the Sultanate of Oman. The company also built a big apartment complex for the officers. This was just a town away from the school where I worked. This was a great miracle of God; it looked as if the Lord got the company to build an apartment for us nearer to my school, though this building was far for all the other workers. If I had to stay with Ernest in the apartment given, I had to get a car and a driver's license. We had never expected that this would come up. Now it would only be 35.5 kilometers / 21.748 miles.

In the current situation, if I had to commute to school every day from the house, I had to get a driver's license. And it was not easy to get that license. The driving instructors were also only Omanis. They would take half the money at the beginning of the driving instructions, and the remaining half after one got the license. I had to change about four such instructors; I wouldn't please them in my behavior, and they would not like to carry on with me, so they would give up on me.

The test was not easy. There were three kinds of tough driving tests we had to carry on, and if we failed in one, we would need to repeat all the tests for the next application. For small faulty reasons, I would fail. Well, I failed ten times and did spend a lot of money. Finally, I went to the top guy and explained to him how the instructors went on failing me several times. I did show him all the records. He finally gave orders to test me on the road and skip all the other tests, which I had passed in the first attempt itself. I did get my license this time.

An elderly man who had to leave Oman all of a sudden did not know what to do with his car. God led him to us, and he left his car key with us, asking us to go pick up the car from where he had parked. We sent the money to him in India on an installment basis. *Great blessings of Jesus! Jesus met my needs.*

New Beginning

By His grace we survived in times of turbulence. Deep impression and admiration of Bedouin on the roads, in the desert, falling prostrate on a spread carpet, all by themselves, without anybody noticing them, was for me like Sadducee worshipping the Lord, even much more than that, in deep reverence to God. This cultivated a thirsty desire in me to worship the Lord in humility and reverence.

I would reach home by 1:00 p.m. from school, and Ernest would reach home at 7:00 p.m. I made it a point to sit on a particular chair for two hours every day, between 4:00 p.m.

and 6:00 p.m., and worship the Lord. My main motivation to worship the Lord was the Bedouin who I saw worshipping in the middle of nowhere. *I began to worship the Lord by underlining all the verses in the Bible that worship God.* A couple of examples are thus:

> Lord of hosts, God of Israel, that dwellest between the cherubims, thou art the God, even thou alone, of all the kingdoms of the earth: thou hast made heaven and earth. (Isa. 37:16 KJV)

> But you, O Lord, are a shield about me, my glory, and the lifter of my head. (Ps. 3:3 ESV)

> As the deer pants for streams of water, so my soul pants for you, my God. (Ps. 42:1 NIV)

> The whole assembly bowed in worship, while the musicians played and the trumpets sounded. When the offerings were finished, the king and everyone present with him knelt down and worshiped. (1 Chron. 29:28–29 NIV)

> The four and twenty elders fall down before him that sat on the throne, and worship him that liveth for ever and ever, and cast their crowns before the throne, saying, Thou art worthy, O Lord, to receive glory and honour and power: for thou hast created

> all things, and for thy pleasure they are and were created. (Rev. 4:10–11 KJV)

> And the four living creatures, each of them with six wings, are full of eyes all around and within, and day and night they never cease to say, "Holy, holy, holy, is the Lord God Almighty...who was, and is, and is to come." (Rev. 4:8 ESV)

> Let the heavens rejoice, let the earth be glad; let them say among the nations, "The Lord reigns!" (1 Chron. 16:31)

I did read through the Bible and underlined all such verses, which helped me to worship the Lord. I would meditate on these verses. I often lacked concentration, but still I would not give up and sat there tightly for two hours. The result of which was glorious. I would enjoy the presence, peace, and awesomeness of God. After my worship time, I would cook for the day, refresh myself, and wait for Ernest for dinner. Each of us had a list of names for prayer. We would sit together to pray for all those who were in the lists. We named this fellowship as a triangular fellowship. Jesus in between us both. Hallelujah!

One such evening, after experiencing the peace and ecstasy of my Jesus, I went to refresh myself. Instead of turning the hot and cold water, I turned only the hot water in the bathtub. The heat was unbearable. As I fell into the bathtub, it fell on my legs, and the legs were burned. The more I tried to get up, the more it heated me and the more times I fell. *For a second, the shower appeared like Satan to me, trying to kill me on the spot. It was just the opposite of the experience of the ecstasy I spent with Jesus. My fear was in my nerves.* I screamed for help. It was just 6:45 p.m., and Ernest normally came home at 7:00 p.m. But that day, he was already in! He lifted me. Isn't my Jesus awesome?

The joy of worshipping the Lord for two hours led me to worshipping him the whole night, listening to worship songs. I worshipped the Lord likewise for many nights. Amazingly, I went to work the next day without a wink of sleep. I spent many nights thus worshipping the Lord and interceding for others. Interceding for others with groaning was a little tough, as it was slightly difficult to bear the groaning when compared to worshipping the Lord. I also learned what it was to worship the Lord in truth and Spirit.

John 4:23–24 (ESV) says, "But the hour is coming, and is nowhere when the true worshipers will worship the Father in spirit and truth, for the Father is seeking such people to worship him. God is spirit, and those who worship him must worship in spirit and truth." To worship Him in truth, for me, was to worship Him by keeping myself truthful and sinless; to worship Him in Spirit was to wait for His words to speak out of me, in prayer, from the bottom of my heart in words. I would exactly know the difference in my prayers from my mind and my heart.

It was an amazing experience to know that I sometimes would pray till three in the morning, and Ernest, who is an early bird to rise, would get up at 3:00 a.m. and have his quiet time with the Lord as well. We would have neither discussed this nor speak or plan on it. It would go unnoticed. Between the both of us, we would have prayed all night. It was just the Lord's doing and the Lord's desire to spend time with us.

Jesus asked His disciples to watch and pray all night in the garden of Gethsemane, encouraging us to have prayer meetings all night as well. We had a set of migrant labor workers and some nurses, great intercessors, who also desired to pray all night, and they prayed with us. So, we had fixed days of the month to pray all night. We would clap and sing to our hearts' content and then keep praying, pouring our hearts to our Lord. We would hear the migrant workers calling out to Jesus by saying, "Hallelujah!" now and then. What a glorious time! Will we ever get it back? Never! But perhaps in heaven.

There was one particular night I remember when the Lord spoke to me very clearly. After, we came back from a Bible study in the night; I decided I would spend the night with Jesus; praying. I never knelt and prayed I'd rather sit on a chair and pray, fall prostrate, or lie down on the bed when I prayed. I prefer to pray to lie on my stomach on the bed, relaxed. My concentration is at its highest peak while I relax on the bed. One day, as I came to my bed with a determination that I would pray all night, I heard Jesus telling me, "I know what you want to pray. Go to bed." Period. I went to bed and was fast asleep.

When Ernest had to change his visa from the old company to the present company, as per the rules of immigration, he had to exit the country. We could do anything on earth boldly, but when it came to the issue of our separation, we were highly nervous. God honored this, and God made a provision even for this. Ernest did go to exit the country for the renewal of the visa, and as he went to the exit gate, it so happened that a top official was there. He saw the ticket and asked Ernest why he was exiting only for six days. Upon coming to know that he was going out for renewal of the visa, the officer, who understood the issue, told Ernest not to exit but to get back to the wife, and the "exit seal" was put on the passport. *How else can we praise God but to humbly bow before Him in reverence for His awesome sovereignty?*

Every year, with the Ministry of Education, we would get two months' holiday with a summer salary paid, and the ticket was given to travel. We had good health insurance also. The king, on his twenty-fifth Ascension Day, gave us two months' extra salary. We bought a keyboard for our church and a necklace for myself!

Ernest would go for Bible studies after his work and come home. It was easy for him to go directly after his work because the place where the Bible study was held was nearby his office of work. One such night, when he came home, his body temperature was a little warm. This happened whenever he was too tired. We then wondered if there was any meaning in working so hard. Ernest need not have to work for two masters, one for the Lord Jesus Christ, and another for the company for which he worked. We had no option to leave the Lord's work. It was mandatory.

Therefore, we decided that he had to quit the job and do only the Lord's work. Perhaps I would never have married a pastor, but the Lord prepared me to encourage Ernest, and perhaps Ernest would have found it difficult to decide by himself. God had prepared me to encourage him. Praise the Lord! He got us all for Himself. My Jesus got us to Himself. Sold out to our Jesus, who sold Himself for us.

We decided to go to India during vacation times every year to visit our families, especially our parents. On one such occasion, we met our mentor, the president of the Indian Evangelical Mission. While Ernest worked as an engineer in India, he was a board member of the Indian Evangelical Mission. The president knew Ernest and me well from our youthful days. Most of the leaders of evangelical organizations had felt that Ernest had a definite calling for the mission work. But it was a difficult decision for Ernest to consider that. When we met the president this time, Ernest expressed his calling for mission work. The president took this as an opportunity and said, "Let me know when you decide on it." He also asked Ernest to work for Indian Evangelical Mission when he decided. If such a thing worked out, I volunteered to sponsor Ernest's work with my salary.

We got back to our country of work. The longing desire of Ernest was always to study theology. We both wanted to move from the Sultanate of Oman to the United States to study theology. We applied for Fuller Seminary, which was a dream of Ernest. That was very expensive to complete the course; therefore, we tried Canada. Ernest did get admission in Canada. The cost of the complete theological course was equal to a one-year study of Fuller theology. Next was to apply for the visa, and when we applied for the visa, the immigrant office of Canada did not believe why an engineer had to do theology.

Therefore, we requested the president of the Indian Evangelical Mission of India to give us a letter saying we would be working for him in India after the course. He did give us the letter, but he also gave another letter saying that we were chosen to serve the Lord in Oman itself. The embassy of Canada was in Kuwait, not in the Sultanate of Oman. Therefore, they wrote to us, saying they would come to Oman to interview us. When the invasion of Kuwait took place, under Iraqi president Saddam Hussain, on August 2, 1990, the embassy of Canada disappeared, and till today, we do not know where our papers disappeared.

We discussed the same with our friends in Oman. We prayed. They believed that Ernest needed no theology course since he was good at his knowledge of the Bible and his Bible studies were excellent. The church also knew that Ernest was acceptably serving the Lord as an engineer. They easily accepted the proposal of the people; they should give him a visa and do all the needful. They were not going to give the salary, as I would be continuing to work, and the Interserve India, seconded by Indian Evangelical Mission, would take charge of the details.

Church of Oman is a dual-chaplaincy church, so the bishop of the Anglican church and the head of the Reformed Church of America and the head of the Interserve of Middle East met in Cyprus to discuss about. The only condition the head of the Reformed Church of America had was that we needed to have a four-wheel drive to do our job on riverbeds and mountains. The Mustard Seed Foundation was helpful right on time to provide the money to buy a four-wheel drive. "But my God shall supply all your need according to his riches in glory by Christ Jesus" (Phil. 4:19 KJV).

Ourselves

Now that Ernest was no longer working in the company that he worked at, He had to give up the house and the visa of that company. The church had to give him the visa, based on their decision in Cyprus. Interserve decided to pay the petrol, the telephone charges, and the house rent. The house rent they gave was a bit too much. After a considerable prayer time, God helped us to decide to rent two houses for the same amount.

The house at Baraka, with three huge rooms, was nearer to my working place and helped us to travel to the northeast inland of Oman.

The house at Sohar was eight-bedroom. This helped us to travel to the northeast of Oman. The rent was very low because it was abandoned—nobody wanted to live there. Sometimes I wondered if it was haunted. For a while we could hear all kinds of sounds around the outside, though not inside the house.

It had four date palm trees on the east side of the house. The landlord would come once in a while to water the trees and also to collect the dates when the trees yielded. There was another beautiful house in the west side of the house, but nobody lived there. That helped us to conduct all-night prayers in a room on the west side, which we had called a prayer room. We could park about four cars in the front yard.

We had to now start house churches all over inland and in the coastal area of northern Oman. The task was not simple, but what helped us was some friends who lived in the interior who were already known to us as we were visiting them with our friends. They were of great help.

The lifestyle of Ernest changed quite a bit. He did not have to go to his work as an engineer; he was now a missionary! Ever since I'd known Ernest, I knew one of the most important things about him. He would get up very early in the morning to have a quiet time with the Lord. Sometimes during the night time, I would see him out of the bed, sitting somewhere, praying, and also snoring.

To begin the full-time work for Jesus, Ernest started fasting. He would fast from Friday afternoons to Sunday afternoons, with one or two cookies in the night. He would fast the whole of Ramadan time along with the Muslims, praying for them. On Lenten days, he would fast again. In case the Lenten days came after the Ramadan days, Ernest would continue to fast till Easter. This would worry me a lot regarding his health. I would consult doctors regarding it. They would never support me but would always be silent over the issue.

Invariably, when Ernest fasted from Friday afternoons to Sunday afternoons, I would be mildly sick. A couple of examples would be, either I would have an upset stomach one week, and another week I would have a little bit of headache. It was very strange, though, a torturous experience, and I wouldn't sleep the whole night. We did share this with our senior pastor, an American from the Reformed Church of America. The mild attacks of the evil one did not bother me anymore after he prayed over me. Praise the Lord!

Ernest would spend time with God on weekdays till eleven in the morning, and in the evenings. We would go to the mission fields every day. I would always accompany Ernest, for he had to meet nurses for prayer and he preferred that I go with him.

I would go to work in the mornings and be back home at 1:00 p.m., have lunch, and take some rest, then be ready to go with Ernest in the evenings. I would cook on Fridays and Saturdays for the week.

Ernest felt that cooking was a bit too much for me, as I was busier than him. He preferred to cook, not knowing how to cook. Every day was a variety of cocktail dish ever tasted in life. I had to say, it was very tasty, lest I was afraid he would be discouraged. He would call himself a chef in purest Sanskrit.

Initially, we did not know how to go about finding out the Christians in the community. We met people in banks, post offices, and hospitals. Ernest was not to mingle with the locals. He could reach out to only the expatriates, as per the regulations of the country.

The towns and wadis, flash flood, riverbeds in mountainous area that we chose to build house churches in reaching out to the Christian population in the interior of Oman, all over, with prayer and with God's guidance, were as listed below.

The towns on the east coast and the inlands that we were expecting to reach out were Barka, Muladha, Musanna, Suwayq, Khaburah, Tharmaid, Bidaya, Rustaq, Nakhal, Sham, Suhar, Sur, Ibri, Izki, Ibra, Bahla, Nizwa, and Buraymi.

Some of the mountainous places were Wadi Bani Ghafar Hospital, Wadi Mistal Hospital, Wadi Hibi Hospital, Wadi Sahatan, and Wadi bani Kharoos.

We Move On

Barka

Every day was a chance to begin again. Looking to get out of our comfort zone and start our lives all over again, passing on the inner peace and love of Jesus by being mindful of Him, who loved us and gave Himself to us, and through mindfulness, experiencing a life of fellowship, we moved on.

We met several Christians, most of whom were Catholics. They were excited to know that we would be having a Bible study in our house since we had three big rooms. Apart from these rooms, we had a long wide passage and a comfortable kitchen. We could use one big hall for the Bible study, the other one as our bedroom, and the third one for Sunday school for children, and also, we used it as a guest room.

We met a couple in the post office in Barka. Knowing their Christian name on the postal address, Ernest spoke to them. They needed prayers very badly as their situation was bad. Their company went on loss, and they did not get their salary for several months. They were Catholics. To top it all off, the lady's brother was suffering from cancer. They desperately needed prayer. They visited us, and we prayed together. The Lord began to work miracles in their lives.

They, in fact, started a child-care center. Sad to say, her brother fell asleep in the Lord. This couple was the most key persons for the Barka Bible fellowship. One night, they came home saying their son was not good in studies. Their son was a highly intellectual person. He would often correct me if I went wrong in the Sunday school. The Lord did honor our prayers, and he is now a high professional in America. Their daughter is also very well settled in India. Praise God! The Lord honored their sincerity and faithfulness in their worship. After we left

Oman, they continued to serve the Lord in the same town by holding Bible studies in their house. God blessed them in multifold.

There was another guy in his late twenties walking on the road to lodge a complaint with the police. His tools and electrical items given to him by the customers for repair were stolen. He walked as if he walked on fire under his feet, worn out, tired, and haggard. The heat was unbearable, undoubtedly 103 degrees Fahrenheit.

Ernest had an urge to pick him up from the road onto his car. It was a divine inspiration and an appointment. This guy told Ernest that he was a Christian. Ernest brought him home. I asked him if he knew the Lord's Prayer, just to check him, if he was really a Christian. It was good to listen to him narrating the Lord's Prayer in his mother tongue. Ernest and he became great friends. This guy was an electrician. His job was just to fix the spoiled radios and TVs. He was on call for the people, and if something went wrong with the electricity, he would go fix it for them. He was poorly paid. There was another friend for Ernest in the capital of Oman. He was a manager in a dairy company, and Ernest requested him to get a job for this new friend in his company. This boy proved to the company as a high intellectual and so was given good promotions. He knew the scriptures well. He dreamt about the future some nights. He would also tell us not to pray all the time and disturb God!

Next, his parents found a girl for his marriage. Ernest and he would go on and on in repetition of the rehearsal of the wedding. They always prayed together, asking for the blessings of the living Lord Jesus Christ. Well, the boy got married in

India. The companies in Oman would give visas to the spouses only for the officers. His new bride had studied master's in English literature and master's in education. She came on a visit visa, and it was great to host them in our house for three months. She tried to get a job as a teacher in the Ministry of Education, but she was not successful in getting one. Sad to say, she had to get back to India, leaving her newly wedded husband.

After his wife left for India, one fine day, he found a big, huge TV near a garbage bin. He took it home, got it all fixed. Went back to a shop next to that garbage bin and asked the shopkeeper if he knew whom the TV belonged to. The shopkeeper did show him a very big villa in the distance. He took the TV to the house. The minister of education lived there. Surprised to see his TV working well, he asked him what he wanted as a reward for the good work he did. He told him about his wife, who needed a job, and immediately the job was given to her, with a ticket to travel to Oman. What a blessing of God!

We met another gentleman in the grocery shop. We asked him what his name was. After some conversation with him, we told him about the Bible study that we had in our house. He was hesitant to come to our house and attend the Bible study, as he did not know who we were. His friend who worked in the same office happened to meet us, and we discovered in our conversation that he was from our own hometown back in India.

Both these gentlemen started attending the Bible study in our house. The gentleman who was from our hometown was also very useful to us in driving to some other towns for Bible study. The gentleman whom we met in the grocery shop shared with us his desire to bring his wife to Oman, but he did not have a family accommodation. We welcomed him to our house with his wife. It was a great opportunity to have them both in our house, to pray with them and enjoy the dinner and lunch together. After three months of their stay in our house, they said they had found a home opposite to our house, and also, God blessed them with a baby girl. Praise God for the family and His blessings on them!

Our Barka fellowship group had more Catholics than Protestants. The pianist was a Catholic, a great musician and singer. His wife and children joined the group a little later than him. Initially, she helped me in the Sunday school; she didn't wish to attend the Bible study, but later on she desired to go to the Bible study, and nothing could prevent her from that. I had a little bit of understanding that the family relationship improved a lot after they attended the Bible study. Thus, every family was blessed.

While Ernest did the Bible study, I would do Sunday school for the kids. My class would be a mixture of all ages below twelve years. I would enjoy narrating Bible stories in a way two-year-old children would be amused while listening. Naturally, the older kids would also enjoy it. When they went to their study time, I would teach them the Bible story in detail, while the younger kids colored the picture. We enjoyed singing, "I am happy today, I am happy today. In Jesus Christ I am happy today. He has taken my sins away. In Jesus Christ I am happy today." We could feel the happiness in all of us saturating our spirits. Praise God! Another breathtaking song for them was,

"When the Spirit of the Lord is within my heart, I will dance like David danced." The joy of the Spirit coming, and the joy of exuberant dance, was felt by the kids while they danced too. Every child would experience the spirit of praise every Wednesday while they choreographed the song:

I just want to praise You
Lift my hands, say I love You
You are everything to me
And I exalt Your holy name
I exalt Your holy name
I exalt Your holy name on high
O I just want to praise You
Lift my hands and say I love You
You are everything to me
And I exalt Your holy name
I exalt, I exalt, I exalt
(Terry MacAlmon)

We had Awana for the kids. It was amazing to watch kids eight to ten years memorizing about ten to fifteen verses and narrating them to me on Wednesdays. They would say them faster than I could follow them in reading. *Their most important prayer was, "Jesus, bless Lalitha auntie and uncle and help them to talk about Jesus to the whole of Oman."* Such untaught prayers would overtake me by surprise. After having taught in the school during the daytime, to handle about twenty-plus children in a room for two hours was not an easy thing, but my sweet Jesus helped me to enjoy teaching them, taking care of them, in silence and confidence, all by myself—none of the ladies would help me, as they would like to attend the Bible study, which I appreciated. I would make the most mischievous child sit next to me; with an embrace of love, I would silence him.

It was not easy to understand the problems and the strange behavior, worse than depression on people who shared them with us. They were more than a fiction. The doctors could not seek out the problems. I started asking God to give us all the gifts of the Holy Spirit if that was what we needed. I asked God to give me all the gifts needed to sort out the issues of the friends who were suffering with unusual issues. I found a book on tongues. I stared reading it, but Ernest was preaching coincidentally on the gifts of the Holy Spirit. He took the book I was reading and started reading it. We were sitting in two different rooms. Ernest told me that he could not go further in reading the book or in preparing as he stood up, talking in tongues. I, who was sitting in another room, as I was praying, started talking in tongues. From then on, I have enjoyed the ecstasy of speaking in tongues all to myself. Sometimes while praying in a group, I would take on speaking in tongues, unaware of myself. As I have not obtained the gift of interpreting, I would stop praying loudly and would start to speak to God within myself.

We did believe even in children giving offerings to the Lord. Therefore, we would take an offering. I can never forget a little girl of two years who put an offering faithfully. As she was going out at the end of the Sunday school, she stood at the door, not moving, while her sisters explained to me that she wanted her money back to take it home! That was a great fun for me to watch. How cute the little girl was, knowing the value of money!

We lived on the first floor of a huge building owned by a respectable elderly Omani gentleman. He owned a halwa (a kind of sweet dish) factory, which was famous for its taste in Oman. After the Bible study was over, our friends who attended came down the staircase. Since it was raining, they could not go to their cars. They were good singers in the group, and so they sang Christmas carols on the ground floor near the staircase, for it was Christmas time. The people who lived on the ground floor near the staircase were Muslims. They were annoyed.

The next morning, we had to move to another place for Bible study. As we were going half a distance, we could hear some kind of a tearing sound in the car. As we moved on, we heard another sound. When we heard the sound for the third time, Ernest got down to see what it could be—the brand-new tire on the front wheel was slowly giving up! We were driving on a freeway; the speed was 120 kilometers per hour! It was God who protected us. We also had a teacher with us who testified, saying how God was with us and how He protected us. A brand-new tire had no way of giving up unless somebody had made a slit on it.

On a fine morning, when I came down to go to my work, I found my car's windscreen was nicely smeared by eggs that dried up well. There was no hose pipe to wash it off, so it took some time to wipe it and drive to my school.

This time, we decided to go inform the landlord. When we told him, being an Omani Muslim, he took it very well and sympathized with us a lot. He knew we Christians met there and worshipped Jesus. He was quite happy about it and did respect us a lot for doing it. That was the end; the people did not repeat to trouble us anymore.

A senior nurse who got us introduced to other staff in the hospital and invited them to the Barka fellowship fell sick. Her left hand was severely in pain. The doctors could not diagnose what the problem was. She was then admitted to another, faraway hospital in Mathura. We went to visit her. She was lying on the bed, perhaps under painkillers. We decided to pray for her. As I went near to pray for her, the Lord seemed to tell me that I was standing on a holy ground and therefore I should remove my sandals. Then again, *I felt the Lord had anointed me to pray for her; hence, I should cover my head. So, I did remove my sandals and covered my head and prayed for her. We said goodbye to her and left.* When we went near our car, which was parked on the parking lot, we noticed our tire was punctured. I cannot remember now how we made it home. The next day, we heard the sister in the hospital was healed. Praise God! Our God is a miracle working God.

There was another senior and head nurse in the same hospital who always proclaimed her faith in Jesus and attended our Barka fellowship. She was recognized in the hospital as a very prayerful lady. People also believed that miracles happened when she prayed. Once, a mullah, a Muslim priest, came to her hospital and was going around and around her chair. When asked if he needed medicine, he said he wanted prayers and not the medicine. Praise the Lord!

I had a beautiful, slim, cute Sunday school girl in the Barka fellowship, most probably about the age of twelve. There were two other girls along with her of the same age. This cute little one was an expert in dancing; give a music to her and she would make a beautiful choreography. I had plenty of lovely CDs relevant to Christmas and Easter. I would pick up one with great meaning and give it to her, and she would make magic on it and teach simple, meaningful actions to it. All three of these girls were of the same height, and with simple, colorful cloth pieces on their dress, they would look fantastic, and along with the musical CDs I gave them, they would perform an extraordinary dance. Small children would put up shows and enjoy the festival season. *Many hospital staff members and locals would attend and enjoy the delicious Indian cuisine and come to know why Christians celebrate Christmas.*

There was another nursing staff. Her husband did not have a job in Oman, but it was a great blessing in foreign countries to live with their spouses. She had decided to go to India to deliver her first baby girl. She had to leave her husband behind because he was not on a worker visa. It so happened one night, while he was sleeping, he choked and died. It was diagnosed after his death that he had throat cancer. The sister came back with her baby girl, in tears. Life was tough for her in Oman. She would say that she smelled the aroma of her husband in her room back in India on the day he fell asleep in the Lord. After some years of loneliness, she had another marriage proposal from a gentleman who also had children and whose wife was no more. The little girl was also taken care of very well by this gentleman, and now she has a doctorate in pharmacy and is happily married in the USA. The family lives in United States.

My School

The prayer that the Lord gave me those days was, "Lord, let all those who see my face see You." Is it too difficult for my Lord to answer this prayer? The Lord gave me an assurance that, provided I kept myself holy and walked in His Spirit, He would touch all those whom I touched and smiled at as I walked along the corridors of my school.

From my home, the school where I worked was about two miles only. I was teaching the local girls of twenty-plus years, after high school and before university, to the professional courses.

The principal of the school was a very young local Omani lady. She was just in her thirties. She captured a lot of my admiration. I adored her capacity in her wise administration. She was a very quiet lady, never raising her voice and never getting into any kind of confusion or misunderstanding among her staff or her colleagues from other schools.

There was a time when the school bus drivers were nationalized. All the expatriates were sent home. The local Omani guys were not educated but were skillful drivers. They were not very happy with the bus scheduling. They came to her with a loud voice to discuss the issues. The guys were not sober; they raised their voices. She felt that she was not a match for them in conservation, for there was no sense in what they were saying. Whatever she told them, they would not understand. So, she called the local elderly Omani ladies who were the helpers in the school in cleaning, equally not educated, to answer all their queries and left the place. The elderly Omani ladies could very well satisfy them; as the drivers shouted, they also shouted at them in the same pitch, and the drivers left the place satisfied.

She came to know that the girls had planned to absent themselves from the school a day before their Eid festival holidays. She asked the lady physical education instructor to announce in the assembly that those who would be absent themselves one day before the holidays would be suspended for three days after they got back to the school. It happened so that the girls were absent. When they came back, they were asked by the physical education instructor to come forward, and they were sent back home. A bus was also arranged to take them back home.

I had two hours to teach in the same class, and again another class was given to me to the same class. I was given an extra one more hour in the same class because the teacher supposed to take the class was absent. I did not know if I had to teach again or send them for games, which I could not do without her permission, so I sent a girl to find out what the principal would like us to do that hour. The principal told her, "Go do what your teacher wants you to do." I felt that was a great administration.

Sometimes I would get calls from the Ministry of Education asking if I would like to teach in the teachers' training institute. I would be happy to do that because it was my basic profession, and also, I would get a call if I would like to be the inspector of the schools, because I was inspecting the schools while in India as a teacher educator. The principal of the school was never sending me, as she needed me to teach the final-year pre-university students; the pre-university course was a three-year course.

I was the head of the department of English in that school. I had a colleague who, I think, was disliked by the students. The students reported their dislike to the principal, and the inspectors of the school also came to know about it. The principal saw that she was transferred to another school. The teacher was not happy about that. She assumed it was I who complained about her to the inspector and had her transferred to a far-off school. That was totally wrong. But this teacher yelled at me. I came home with tears. Ernest would only say all this shouting at me could only be instigated by Satan, and so I didn't have to cry for it. Later on, I came to know that it was the principal who was responsible for the transfer, for she told me students did not appreciate her sitting and teaching.

She would often tell me that God had sent me to the school. I am not sure why she said so. Finally, when I had to resign from my job, while she acknowledged my resignation, she said in a firm voice, "You want to go, you go."

After a few years of my leaving the job as a teacher with the Ministry of Education, I heard the young principal died in a road accident.

Students

Studying religion in Oman is a must in Oman. They would study Islam, the Qur'an, and the birth and life of Jesus. They believe in the virgin birth of Jesus, miracles, and the crucifixion of Jesus as a great prophet, but not His death and resurrection. They wondered why a great prophet like Him would have to die such a cruel death. My students were a very nice bunch of sweet girls. My favorite word while I taught was habibthi, meaning "my love." These girls did like that word too. One particular girl was talking a lot and disturbing the class once. I just stared at her. She called me habibthi, came running, and hugged me; it was a great fun for the entire class.

The school timings were from 7:00 a.m. to 1:00 p.m. They would assemble in the courtyard for the Morning Prayer and the news reading. Every morning they would read the Qur'an. We, the teachers, would have to stand next to our classes while the reading went on. English teachers would not normally be the class teachers. Only a few girls were chosen as the Qur'an readers. During that period, I would just keep praying for all of them in the name of Jesus. I would consider myself as a watchman keeping the school, the girls, and the staff safe for Jesus only.

Every day before I went to work, Ernest and I would commit ourselves for the day's work ahead. Only the Lord needs to work miracles. It was a tough job to preach Jesus there, but the Lord, even at those tough situations, would positively work wonders in answer to our prayers. He would then work through me and reach out with His power of salvation. I have not seen bearing that fruit, but I trust in Him, for whoever I desired to be saved, in the will of God, would be saved. It is His will that all should come to know Him and none should perish. Praise the Lord! Is that a big prayer for the Lord to answer? Nothing is too difficult for the Lord.

I was teaching English as second language for the final-year students of post-high-school students. After high school, they had to study for three years before they went to the university. I was always asked to teach the third-year girls. On a school morning, as I entered the classroom, I saw all the twenty-plus-year-old students crying. I wondered why. When I asked them why they did so, one by one they started to tell me that I should become a Muslim; a nice person like me should become a Muslim, for they wanted to see me go to heaven and be with them there.

I was stuck as a sting of scorpion, but for a second, I did not know what I should say. After a while, I just lovingly reminded them that we teachers had three strict rules to follow while teaching. One being we should not discuss with students in the class politics. Secondly, we should not discuss with them about religion, and thirdly, we should not discuss about our families.

Then I did tell them that they should be assured that I would go to heaven, as Jesus died for me as a great sacrifice to forgive my sins. And I have Jesus as my Savior, who has forgiven my sins, and I would be going to heaven because only shed blood can give life. They said it was a cruel death for Jesus to go through. The concept of sacrifice of animals and why the greatest sacrifice of sinless Jesus for the forgiveness of our sins is so very important had to be explained. I had to conclude by saying, if they still insisted, I might have to tell that to the principal of the school. I had a strong feeling that the religious Muslim teacher must have instigated them to say this. In any case, the Lord, the Holy Spirit, gave me an opportunity to tell them what I would think of my way of going to heaven. Praise the Lord!

Many times, the teachers and the students, while not in the classrooms, had asked me when I prayed whether I prayed or not, when I fasted whether I fasted or not, and why I didn't cover my head, as all Muslims cover their heads. This was always a great opportunity to tell them about myself.

I would tell them that I do not cover my head because I would like the men to think of me as their sister while they had their own wives at home. I do fast, but it is a secret between me and my Jesus. Jesus has told us not to go around telling others about our fasting, unless it encourages others to fast. It is not good for me to tell others and boast about it. I would pray, perhaps all the time, when I walk and do my work silently, but I would also pray timely prayers at home. My relationship with Jesus is a secret between me and God, and it is very special. They would be extremely happy about what I say. They would keep saying, "Sah, sah," which means "true, true."

School Inspector

A cute Omani inspector, an elderly gentleman, of course with a long beard, I suppose, was liked by one and all. He was only an inspector for Arabic and teachers of religion, but he would walk around the school corridor to see if all the teachers were well dressed. He was very particular that every teacher, whether Muslim or non-Muslim, should wear the headscarf. If the teacher didn't wear the headscarf, he would say, "Haram," (sinful) or he would say, "Satan is in the class" and "Get off the class." Even to me he had said Satan.

Once, I discussed with him very respectfully that it was difficult for us non-Omanis to wear headscarves because of the heat, and also, we were not used to it. I'm not sure if he understood, for he did not know English. In any case. I did not want to displease him, so I kept a scarf permanently in the cupboard, and whenever he came, I wore it. It so happened one day; he came to the examination marking hall—perhaps he was not to come there. The cupboard where I had kept the scarf was in the staff room. All I could do was pick up a black abaya/gown of a Muslim friend and cover my head with it. I think he saw me struggling with it for it was falling down several times from my head since it was made of heavy silk. He could not help but laugh as he walked away. Since then, he never said anything to me, nor did he come where I was.

Teachers

I was teaching English as a second language. I would draw stick figures, flowcharts, and grids on the blackboard and enjoy my teaching. I would make my students repeat the language elements and the structures using grids and learn in a playful manner. My students enjoyed all my stick figures on the board. And sometimes, though I did not know proper Arabic, I would narrate the story in Arabic. I appreciated the students listening to me in all seriousness; they would never laugh in spite of me making several grammatical mistakes and pronunciation errors.

Many of the staff members were from Egypt. Some from Tunisia, Sri Lanka, and India. Tunisians and Egyptians taught core subjects, while Indians, Sri Lankans, and Pakistani teachers taught English as second language.

I did have a very good relationship with all the teachers. One Pakistani lady English teacher was full of fun. She would collect all the pencils and pens found around the school. She would keep a load of them in her drawer, and whenever she wasn't there, we would help ourselves. She knew that well. When nothing was found in the drawer, she would just put her tongue out. We would enjoy her looks, having a good laugh. She always said, wherever there was love, she would be there. And Love was her name. Finally, when she was quite elderly, she found the love of her soul. He was an elderly Pakistani gentleman and was quite handsome. Nothing much is known about his family back at home. He must have had a family back in Pakistan, but for Muslims, it was not a big issue. They can remarry. She was very happy to marry him and did have happy days with him.

He suddenly had a heart attack. We visited him at the hospital and also at their house. When we went to their house, we were taken straight to his room, where he was lying down. We were surprised to see a cross over his head on the wall. He said religion has to be a personal one. One has to decide to which religion he or she belonged. He said nobody should be bound by religious bondage. He also believed in the resurrection of Jesus. We couldn't talk to him much that day, as he was sick. We never saw him after that. But we were very much encouraged to hear what he thought of religion.

Another teacher, from Tunisia, had no children, even after having been married for several years. She would ask me to pray for her. Tunisia is a Muslim country where it was unconstitutional to marry more than one wife. They were also not necessarily asked to cover their heads. She would always ask me to pray for her to get a child. I remember on an early morning, I had a dream that her husband was on the telephone in the hospital with his family back in Tunisia and he was full of joy. When I met her in the school, I told her about my dream. I was not really surprised when she told me that she was pregnant. What a God we serve, revealing all His plans! Maybe He gave me this dream to tell that teacher it was He who answered the prayers and reveled it to me to make it clear to her that her request for prayer was answered.

An elderly teacher from Egypt amused me a lot. She loved her students and was always very conscious of their progress in studies. She was very particular to see that she had 100 percent results in her classes. So, during the marking, grading the answer scripts, she would sit with two pens, one a red pen, and another a blue or black one, as per the answer scripts. If the answers were wrong, she would correct them with blue pen and then mark them right with a red pen to give them full mark. She wouldn't listen if we told her not to do that. This made us laugh a lot.

The school social worker was an Omani lady. She was a very good friend of mine. She was married but did not have children. She always shared with me about her sorrow of not having a baby. I told her that I knew of a very good gynecologist. She agreed to go along with me. On a beautiful day, we approached the doctor. On hearing the problems of my friend, the doctor said it could be impossible for to her to help my friend to get a baby; nevertheless, she would try. After visiting that particular doctor, my friend did have twins. Her joy knew no bounds. After two years, she had another set twin babies.

An excellent teacher from Tunisia loved India a lot. She would say that her dream was to visit India, and one day she would do that. She started asking for a Bible. She never asked me to give her one—perhaps she was afraid of me, because she knew I was a pastor's wife. She was asking my colleague to give her one. Being a Christian, she would consult me, and we would tell her that we were not interested in giving Bibles to Muslims, as it was forbidden. Though we sincerely longed to give one. We would delay this request at least for three days and finally give in.

A great friend of mine in the school was from Sudan. She always took me away from the crowd and shared all her secrets and requested me to pray for her on the spot itself. Her story stretches beyond Oman to Sudan. Since her youth, she had fallen in love with a male teacher. When the time of marriage came, the parents on both sides did not approve of the love, and therefore they could not marry each other. After a few years passed, she was given in marriage to another man. She could not lead a deeper married love relationship with her husband. She worked for the government of Sudan, in the Department of Education, which of course was a transferable job. The most severe blow that she faced was when she was transferred to another school in a teacher's position. She faced her lover sitting in the same staff room. Memories of the past gushed into her being. Once again, the love that was submerged came to the surface. She wanted me to pray that God help her to cope up with the crossroad situation and find a way that would give her a peaceful destination.

I used to drive to my school. Every day I would pick up another Sudani English teacher and also drop her back. I had a few Arabic cartoon books on Old Testament heroes, which I presented to her young daughter. I never knew that in the foot note, there was all about Jesus. We were not supposed to give such books to Muslims. The next day, when I met her, I told her that I did not notice about footnotes on Jesus and I was sorry about that. I said this mainly because I did not want her to think I had given them the gospel, deceiving that it was only a cartoon book. She immediately told me that they believed in Jesus and not to be sorry about that. One day, after the school, I waited for her to get into the car to take her back home. She came quite late and was very furious as she came. Not sure what argument was there at the school or if somebody irritated her. What she was saying was, "Why should it only be men that could marry twice? Even we ladies can marry too!" She was so upset I could dare ask her what happened.

An elderly Omani lady helped in cleaning the school. One day, I was walking along the courtyard and she was walking across from me. Sometimes, some thoughts rolled over my brain and I would not be aware of whoever was passing by. I passed her without acknowledging her presence. She got angry with me and said, "Why are you not greeting me? Greeting peace is from the Lord." I was ashamed of myself as she said that; peace is from the Lord, and I should give it to her.

A few days later, we crossed paths again, walking along the corridor. She had a cute round face and was also on the heavy side. *I found her face completely scratched in semicircles upside down on both the cheeks, minute thin semicircular scratches, must be about fifty on each cheek.* It was frightening to see her that way. I wondered what it was. Approaching her, I asked her what happened to her. She said the gin (ghost) came to her room while she was sleeping and scratched her face. She also said that she needed to go to her mullah (priest), and by paying about $170, she would get a piece of Qur'an to tie over her neck and the gin would not come near her again.

I promised her that I would be praying in the name of Jesus and the gin would not be coming near her; therefore, it would not be necessary to pay the money. She easily consented to it, as Muslims also believe in the miracles of Jesus. Never again did I see her with those marks on her face. Praise the Lord!

I loved teaching, and because of my educational background and experience in teaching in the college of education, I was able to modify the methodology as per the principles of teaching English. I believed repetition of structural elements of language should be made easy and interesting. Therefore, I had a variety of teaching modules with different kinds of grids and flowcharts that helped students learn the language with ease and fun. The Ministry of Education wanted all those materials, for them to have a look at it.

Al Musanna

The next town to Barka was Musanna. There were three fellowships meetings built up in this town.

a. Hospital nurses
b. Private clinic workers
c. Businesspeople in the town

The Hospital Nurses

The hospital nurses met a little farther down the junction called Al Muladda. We met in the house of a staff nurse. Their son was just five years old. He was a very cute son who had already planned whom he was going to marry and how he was going to build his house. He narrated that to everybody who went to their house. The nurses had plenty of issues. Their families were in India. One or two African and Filipino nurses would also attend the meetings. Those who had their spouses would also join them.

We met every Sunday at 6:00 p.m. The fellowship began with great worship of the Lord, with lots of worship songs in their vernacular language. Songs of praise sung from the bottom of their hearts. Clapping of their hands would be the melodious music. After they were fully satisfied in singing, they would worship the Lord in words by quoting scriptures. Then, Ernest would take up the Bible study. Intercession was the most important time, too, as their needs and their family needs were the highlights of the end of the prayer meeting, before Ernest's benediction. Those who could not go to the church because of the long distance were fully satisfied with the fellowship.

Everything went on well for a period of seven years. Police around that place watched people coming and going out of the house regularly on a fixed timing on Sundays. They wanted to investigate. We began to pray, as we did not know what the outcome of that would be. It could have serious consequences, inclusive of repatriations. The senior most staff, who was the leader of the fellowship, was called for explanation. She did tell them the truth and explained their problems of not having a church nearby. The police heard it all and finally told her that they should stop meeting in that place as it was a not a legal place of worship.

The senior staff was quite bold enough. The Lord did give her the words of boldness, and she frankly told the police that if they stopped the prayer, God's curses would be upon them. The police took this very seriously and told them that they could meet with their pastor in the guesthouse of the hospital nurses' apartment. Praise God! As a result of all the prayers and supplication, we were blessed with a beautiful place, not only in this town, but also in another town. Anybody from the hospital was also allowed to join us. Isn't our God a prayer-answering God? His blessings are more than what we ask or think of.

We were also asked from the main church that we be careful not to leave shoes outside the house where we met for the fellowship but to leave them all inside the house. When asked by the public about what was happening in the house, we should tell them that we were meeting for prayer, but not the fellowship or the church service. For them the church service would be in the church buildings, not in the houses. They would appreciate the word prayer, but not fellowship.

We met for all-night prayer in another house upstairs. As we went on praying and worshipping the Lord, waiting on Him to speak to us and fill us with His Spirit, I was sitting in a corner all by myself, tired after the day's work. I was within myself, praying in tongues, when suddenly I heard one of the nursing staff who never attended our Bible study falling on the floor and roaring. Every muscle of the body seemed to be shaking, an unusual kind of behavior. We did recognize that her bodily movements were indicative of demon possession. We prayed, asking Jesus to release her by the power of His blood. In the name of Jesus, we were able to cast out the demon and set her free. If the Son of God sets us free, we are free indeed. The next day, she called me and told me something like a big spider was crawling on her body. I advised her to attend the church regularly, but we never saw her afterward. She worked in the capital, not in the places where we had Bible studies.

There was another couple just opposite the same building. They were Hindus. The gentleman was a son of a Hindu priest. The lady believed in Lord Jesus as her Savior, but the gentleman did not believe in accepting Jesus as his personal Savior, for he was of the opinion that a priest's son should carry on the priesthood after the father. They had a practice of sacrificing animals. Mostly, they said they sacrificed the chicken. In any case, the gospel was given to him and he would attend all the fellowships. The next month, they wanted an all-night prayer in their house.

The next month came, and we did spend the night worshipping the Lord, reading the Word, and hearing a sermon by Ernest. We prayed group prayers as well as individual prayers, but nothing spectacular happened. We just praised God for every prayer and every word that the Lord gave us. We seemed to have gotten a little closer to Him.

One week after our all-night prayer in that house, we went to meet the Christians in Wadi Bani Ghafir Hospital near Rustaq. The nurses were only free after 6:00 p.m. After praying and having a Bible study with them, we had dinner and were getting back. It was not easy for us to get back during the nighttime, where there was no light at all in the wilderness—we had to depend on the moonlight or the car light. Moreover, it was raining. We did lose our way, and to trace back the way to get back to Rustaq was difficult; hence, we took a long time to get back. Since we had two other friends with us, I was a little bit confident to drive down the mountain.

As we entered Rustaq, we left them back in their residence and moved on. It was raining heavily. We passed Rustaq. There was a big wadi, and rainwater was gushing in at the same junction where we had the all-night prayer. There were a set of Omani boys standing on the main road and warning us not to enter the road, leading us to take a turn on the left.

It was one o'clock in the morning. The fear took over us. We couldn't heed to what the Omani boys had said. As we moved into the water, the car got into the deep parts and could not drive further. Ernest had no words to speak; he was spellbound. Because of his weight on the left, the car was tilting onto his left. There was nobody on the road. I didn't even remember the Omani boys, and they were not to be seen. I did not know at that particular time what to be done. So, I slowly got out of the car to see if there was somebody around to help us. The police who normally patrolled on roads were also not to be seen that early-morning hours. When I got out of the car, the water gushed into the car and the car sank a little deeper.

Still, Ernest was just calm—perhaps he was seeking the Lord's help. After I got down, I looked around. Nobody was there, no police and no passersby. None. I saw a pole in the distance. I walked toward it, though I found it very difficult to walk. I could have been easily swept away and would have been no more. Somehow, I managed to hold on to the pole. Suddenly, to my left I found a huge truck coming in. They stopped the vehicle amid the waters.

They looked like four Pakistani men, tall and huge. In their truck they had huge ropes enough to tie our vehicle to their vehicle and drag the car out, though the car was still tilting on the left. Till today, I cannot remember how I got into the car from the pole to which I was holding in the deep waters. The four Pakistani men and their vehicle were not seen also, even to say a word of thanks to them.

We moved on in a wet car, and all our things in it were wet. We never spoke a word to each other. As we came near our house, there was a bridge, and underneath the bridge was a valley. We heard the roaring sound of a huge water canal gushing out. We did not know what to do at the early morning, at two o'clock. We had forgotten all the phone numbers in fear. We stopped. God helped me to remember only one phone number, of the couple who lived in our house for three months, in spite of having many other friends around us. We could have remembered any other. Why only this phone number? They lived just opposite to our house, across the road. They were just like our children. What a wise God we serve!

Those days there were no cell phones as we have now. A few yards away from the place where we had parked the car, there was a telephone booth. We called this friend of ours, and he picked up the phone at that part of the morning, at two o'clock, and came to the place where we were, left our car there itself, took us in his car, then made a nice bed for us, almost like putting us to sleep. He went back to our car and brought it to his house, removed all the water from it, and put all the wet things to dry.

They gave us good breakfast when we came home. We were dazed and fearful. We thought we would never go out of the house. Any puddle of water we saw on the road, we were afraid. We just did not want to go out. It looked to us that if Jesus is real, then Satan is equally real. It appeared that the Satan wanted to kill us both, just in the same place where we had all-night prayer, in the exact corner of the junction. The only difference was, this happened on the ground; the house where we prayed was just above the ground on the first floor.

I was not sure about Ernest. I verbally told the Lord, "Jesus, You do Your work. We are going home." For two days we stayed at home. On the third day, we were lying down and watching David Pawson's video—I can't remember the name of it now. As we were watching, he was talking about communist China and said, "Look out behind the bamboo curtain how Christian believers witnessed there. What are you, a believer?" This was enough for us to say, "Okay, Lord, we are ready."

As I write this, I remember once before, a few months after we began the mission work, Ernest had a severe back pain and he could not do long-distance driving. Our friend gave him a belt to wear, and our doctor said, "You are God's servant. Your God will take care of you." I told the Lord; "God if you want Ernest to continue this work, you will heal this back pain." The lord heard the prayer and Ernest was healed.

The Private Clinic Workers:

The clinic workers worked till 10 pm every day except for Fridays. They were the private nurses and doctors. The only time these doctors and nurses had prayer was at night, ten o'clock. There were two such clinics in Musanna. One clinic had a Hindu lady doctor, and another clinic had a male doctor who was a Christian. There was also a private pharmacist in the same place who worked till 9:00 p.m. or so. His wife worked in another clinic as a nurse. We had weekly Bible studies after 10:00 p.m. for these members. The Hindu lady doctor fully cooperated in allowing us to meet for Bible study in her clinic and always looked forward to it.

On a day after the Bible study, perhaps it was nearing twelve midnight, we took off from there to our house. A few kilometers away, I just remembered that I did not say goodbye to one of our friends, so we decided to get back and bid her goodbye. We got back and said goodbye, then proceeded home. On the way, one Pakistani man overtook us by the car, and in seconds, he hit a huge camel. The camel fell flat on the road, and his car turned around and hit the railing of the other side of the road. Nothing happened to him. He got out of the car, lifted both his hands up, and was praising the Lord. Two main things that we recollected in praising the Lord for protecting us: We went back to say goodbye, which delayed us by two or three minutes. If that was not so, we would have hit the camel. Secondly, the Pakistani man who overtook us and hit the camel was still saved by our sweet Jesus. If that were not so, we would have hit the camel. For a second we felt that the Pakistani who saved us was an angel sent to save us by Jesus Himself. What an amazing God we serve! He gave not only eternal life but also life and His protection on earth to live for Him. Amen.

The Business people in the Town

This group did not meet regularly. The leader of the group was a businessman. He was not an educated man but was a highly intellectual man. He knew the trick of his trade; hence, he made a lot of money. He would invite all his businessmen home for good worship and Bible study and prayer by Ernest, with very good dinner late in the night, as it was customary that they eat their dinner only after the prayer, whatever the time might be. They were great worship singers. Clapping their hands, they would just praise the Lord in their own mother tongue.

Our humble prayer was, "Lord Jesus, whoever heard Your name and witnessed Your healing power, may they come to know the grace of Your redemption. Amen."

There was another Sri Lankan couple. The gentleman was the teacher with the Ministry of Education, and his wife was a homemaker. They were a very nice, sweet tall couple. The husband was a Christian, and the wife was a Buddhist, but both of them liked to come to Thermeid fellowship. Since they did not have a car, we picked them up from Musaan to the Tharmaid fellowship every Tuesdays. One day, they invited us for dinner, and they wanted to express their concern to us.

After dinner was over, the lady said that she had a funny kind of vision. She said, while both of them were seated on the couch, she could see red bubbles coming out from her left side and the green bubbles coming up from her right side, choking her husband. We listened to her and gave her the gospel, told her they should play some worship songs, worshipping Jesus all round the clock in their house. That sorted out the problem. Praise the awesome Lord Jesus! He is the victor of our soul. Amen.

An Indian gentleman who worked as a chef in one of the famous hotels discovered Ernest was the pastor for the interior ministry; therefore, he came home one day with a videotape and complained about his wife, who was working in a famous hospital in Oman, with a high salary. They had twin daughters three years of age. He had to say a lot of unpleasant things about his wife. His main complaint was that she was not sharing her salary with him. He was truthful in whatever he told us. He gave his marriage video to us to keep it safely for him, and he wanted us to make peace with him and his wife.

The story that he told us was very funny. He was married five times. We asked him how he was able to do that. He said prior to working in Oman, he worked in Saudi Arabia. Whenever he went to India on a holiday, he would give an advertisement in the matrimonial column for a wife. He also said that for such an advertisement, there would be a line of girls wanting to marry him, knowing that he was working in the Gulf. He would also give a bottle of beer to whoever got him married.

This was how he got married to the fifth wife and then quickly brought them back with him to the Gulf. Ernest is always a very mild, loving counselor, but I was not so. I would call a spade a spade and fire them nicely. Teachers normally do that. We met this wife of his, and all that she said was he wanted her earnings. The Lord's Word was given to him, but I don't think he cared much. That was the end. He came back to us and took the video and went.

Al Bideya

The Lord helped us to start two house fellowships in Bideya. One for the small-business guys whose families were in India. They were single men. They could not go to India as we could go every year. They made both ends meet by way of small-scale industry. They could still be the source of good education to their children. This fellowship met at 10:00 p.m. every Thursdays. We would attend two other fellowships in two nearby town beginning at 6:00 p.m. and come to this place at 10:00 p.m. They would sing great worships songs in their mother tongue, clapping their hands in rhythmic style. And then Ernest would preach the gospel.

They would never eat before worshipping the Lord. They had lots of issues, of which financial issues were the main. If they had taken loan and not returned it on time, they would even be imprisoned. We would pray hard for them. I have never sensed such groaning of the Holy Spirit within myself while praying for them.

After the fellowship at twelve midnight, they would insist that we have dinner and leave. Perhaps they felt that we took trouble to go all the way at odd hours and they should be kind in providing a meal to us. Moreover, this was Indian hospitality, a culture. It would be 2:00 a.m. by the time we could reach home. I would have gone to work that day and gotten back home at 1:00 p.m. After a nap, I would accompany Ernest to the fellowships. So while returning at 2:00 a.m., I would be very sleepy, and Ernest would have to repeatedly ask me to go to sleep.

As we drove along the lonely straight road—sleepy morning, of course—I was tired and worn out after the day's work. I would sleep a little bit and also open my eyes and look at Ernest now and then. Both his eyebrows would be raised. He would keep his eyebrows raised in order to control himself and keep away from sleeping. He would never agree with me if I told him that he was sleeping. We would just go along our journey home. Perhaps like wounded soldiers, yet being peaceful, we were with those needy ones and also with the Lord, in fellowship with each other.

Suddenly, both of us would have slept, for I would wake up on hearing the tire of the vehicle rolling on the gravel outside the skirts of the road. I would get up and wake up Ernest. Isn't our Jesus faithful enough to protect us from dangerous situations? *"For he shall give his angels charge over thee, to keep thee in all thy ways"* (Ps. 91:11 KJV).

Once, the top Christian guys of Bideya arranged for a huge meeting on the rooftop. There were about seventy people approximately. Ernest was the speaker. As he was speaking, the Holy Spirit led him to talk about drunkenness. The four top guys in the fellowship were very wild at Ernest. Three of them were doctors, and one was a businessman. They thought Ernest intentionally spoke about their drunkenness, knowing they were in the habit of drinking. We heard all kinds of rumors of them rebuking Ernest for giving such a message.

Each one of them had to face certain critical issues. It so happened the Lord spoke to them. All of them were under some kind of crisis, and they had to invite us to their homes to pray for them. It was a good time to share the Lord with them.

We had another fellowship group in the same town for the families. The leaders of this fellowship were highly blessed by the Lord. The sad thing that happened was of a Pakistani couple who were expecting their third baby. On her ninth month, when she was about to deliver, she had a cerebral hemorrhage because of high blood pressure, and by the time they took her to the hospital, the baby had died in her womb. After a few months, he got married to his ex-wife's unmarried sister; he needed somebody to take care of his first two lovely children. Though sad about missing his beautiful, lovely wife, we were yet happy because of his marriage to his ex-wife's sister, who was never married. She found a family. The Lord blessed her. Praise the Lord! All blessings are from Him alone.

Al Thermeid

A little further away from Musanna and Muladda is this small town called Thermeid, which we normally do not see on the map. It is quite a famous town, though precisely a small town. There was a couple in the town who were all excited to have a prayer in their house. They were Srilankans. They have two grown-up children; one is now in Germany, and the other one daughter is in Australia. The gentleman was overenthusiastic and the lady was a deep thinker and was always prayerful and hospitable.

The Bible study was handled in this group by the inspector of the schools who came to know the Lord when he was fifty years of age; it was to encourage him to take up the Bible studies since he always regretted not serving the Lord and he wasted all his past life. All of us were of the same age, and so we did enjoy this fellowship with fun and dinner served by the host and the hostess.

One such day, our host had invited another Srilankan family, without our knowledge. We hardly had time even to discover from where they came. As we started to worship the Lord, the teenage girl sitting opposite to me just fell on the ground with all her hair scattered and rolling on the ground. We started to pray for her. Our host, not knowing what to pray, started saying, "Satan, please go away." That was indeed funny. After a while, she did get up with a smile.

People around this place came to know that miracles were taking place in this place. So one day, a set of Muslim managers from a company brought a Srilankan girl, perhaps about twenty to twenty-six years old. They told us she was not eating for the last three days. *She had told them that she could hear her dead mother's voice.* As we began to pray for her, she fell down but her hair was intact. After a while, she got up with a smile on her face and ate what the hostess gave her. Gospel was preached. All of them left happily.

Those days, a lot of biblical videos were sold in the Bible society in the capital of Oman. Knowing this, our host wanted them one by one as they had telecast in their company for the inmates. When some senior local officers met in that place, they requested us to get them the movie of Jesus of Nazareth. Also, the mullah of the mosque wanted a Bible for discussion in the mosque. *The host stole my Bible and gave it to him. After fifteen days, he gave it back to me with a smile on his face!*

Al Suwayq

This was a gathering for teachers and for the nurses. A senior nurse took the responsibility of inviting all the nurses, and a senior teacher took up the responsibility of inviting all the teachers. We met in the home of an elderly couple. The lady of the house was a senior teacher, and her husband was an elderly man who was just with the wife, supporting her in her work. Most probably, he was a businessman or an Army man. They were quite senior to us. We never asked about their past; neither did they tell us. That is how in Indian culture we would respect elders. We were told that they had two grown-up sons in Oman working in the capital, but we never saw them too.

We remain faithful to them forever. They were Hindus, never raised an objection for the Christians to have fellowship in their house; rather, they were very encouraging. The lady was very much taken up with Ernest for the way he conducted the Bible study, and also, she marveled at him whistling songs and hymns. When our senior American pastor of Reformed Church of America visited this house fellowship, she discovered even he could whistle songs and hymns. The group had a delight when Ernest and our senior pastor whistled "How Great Thou Art" in a duet. That was a treat. Praise the Lord!

They were vegetarians; therefore, they would cook delicious vegetable dishes for us to have after service was over. The gentleman would help his wife in cooking and getting the house ready for the fellowship and would wait outside near the gate to welcome us. He was always neatly dressed in white northern-Indian-style and was anxious to see that all should attend the fellowship. Oh, how we wish to see them in heaven!

We also went to nurses' apartments to visit them, pray with them, and invite them for prayer. We went to one such apartment with a video of the movie of Jesus, and when we saw a Christian Filipino, we gave it to her to watch. Next time when we visited her, she wept bitterly. We did not know why she wept so much. After some days, when we went back again, we asked her why she cried so bitterly. She said she was in love with a Christian Filipino, a married guy. Christians are not supposed to marry again. Islam allows two marriages; therefore, both of them had converted to Islam. After watching the movie of Jesus, she was desperate. *If we confess our sins (guilt), He is faithful and just to forgive us from all unrighteousness.*

There was another elderly Sri Lankan lady teacher in this group who never spoke to us about her husband—a widow perhaps. We were not in the habit of asking people about what they didn't speak of. She had two working daughters in Sri Lanka. One was supportive of her, and the other, we were not sure of her. She always needed our prayer support and was very appreciative of our prayers on her behalf. Praise the

Lord Almighty. Our Lord hears our prayers not only prayed for ourselves but also the prayers that we do on behalf of others.

We teachers who were teaching with the Ministry of Education had to go to the capital to value the answer scripts of the students' examination. I liked the marking system in Oman; perhaps it was the British system. We were not to value the entire paper but only one particular question. One particular room would have several tables in it, and all the tables in that particular room would only value one particular question. For example, room number 5 would correct only the answer of question number 5, and so on and so forth.

The tables in the next room would correct answers of another question. Each table would have a green marker, who is the head of the table and who would check if the marker had done a good job. Each room would also have a blue marker, the head of the room, who would recheck the red marker and the green marker at random. The objective type of questions would be corrected by the lower-class teachers, but the essay type of questions would be corrected only by the final-year teachers.

That particular year, we could only finish at 10:00 p.m. on the final day of our corrections. Some of the Suwayq teachers and the elderly host of the Suwayq fellowship were with us. They had no ways of getting back to their houses. It was only Ernest who had a four-wheel drive. Therefore, all the teachers in our van traveled back to Suwayq after our dinner in a restaurant. It was 2:00 a.m. by the time we reached them.

The elderly host couple insisted on us to sleep in their house and get back in the morning. Ernest was very particular to get back home, whatever the time was, mainly because he had to have his quiet time with the Lord with his own daily readings and his own versions of the Bible. So, we proceeded back home. It was raining, and the wiper of the car fell down. Ernest seemed to have more concern with the wiper than the rain. As we approached our home, we had to turn to the left to enter the factory gate. *When we turned left, we saw our car wiper still safe on the bonnet of the car.* It was a delight. Both of us had a glorious laugh. Our God not only protects us but also protects our belongings. Praise the Lord!

Whenever it rains in Oman, there would be rainwater gushing onto the road from the mountains. They say it comes running from about 150 kilometers. The rainwater floods the roads in such a way that passing through the road becomes very difficult. One such evening, as we were traveling back to our house from the Suwayq fellowship, the water gushed across the road. This time the naughty Omani teenagers advised us to move into the water and get out of it. So, we moved in, and as we were a little slow in the water, a four-wheel drive hit us from the back, and our car was hit badly. Fortunately, the nursing staff and the senior staff who was the leader of the fellowship were also in the car. As per the advice of the senior staff, we went to the hospital for a checkup if everything was physically okay with us. And also, we went to the police station to report the matter so that we would get the insurance after they found the damage of the car. I had a whiplash, while Ernest was fine. We had to go to the hospital to have ourselves checked, after which we returned home at three in the morning.

Al Khaburah

This was a small group of teachers. We met in a teachers' house. About ten of us all in all, with two couples, inclusive of us both. They were from Sri Lanka. I praise God for this group. The single male teacher loved the Lord just as a child would love its dad. He always had simple conversations with the local male teachers and shared it with us. That kind of simple conversations with deep meaning would surprise us and also would convince the listeners. One day, we had a prayer session, where we began to pray for each person, one by one. One of the teachers expressed that she had a very bad headache that would never leave her, whatever she did. I went near her to for pray for her, and as I did, she yelled at me in an altogether-different, unknown language. Immediately, with no seconds left, I also yelled at her in the same pitch, but in a different language unknown to myself. There was a little bit of authoritative voice in me.

After that happened, she was transferred to a mountainous area, and when we went to see her, neither of us spoke about the prayer episode. I had no guts to open the topic either, because of the war that I had waged! The greatest thing that she did for me was to show her love and gratitude by giving me three lovely stones from Sri Lanka, which I have to date. All praises are to my Lord alone! He is the one who heals all our diseases. By His stripes we are healed.

We had a very good friend from India working in Oman. She and her husband were great friends of ours. They were both teachers. We, as a team with other good friends of ours in the capital, were going to the interior to fellowship with the interior Christian community, even while Ernest was an engineer. This lady friend of ours brought another Moroccan lady teacher to the church who experienced tremendous peace in the church and believed in the Lord Jesus Christ.

She had no peace for several days as the postage from Morocco was always delayed. She had not heard from the family for quite some time. She lived in a ladies' hostel. I went to her hostel to visit and gave her the gospel and a Bible. The next time I visited her, she let me in from the back door. She told me that she would read the Bible at one o'clock in the morning, lest the others mistook her. All her inmates were from Egypt and were single lady teachers. The next time I went to see her, she wasn't there, and the next academic year, she wasn't to be found or heard. Perhaps her contract with the Ministry of Education was over or she did not get back to work.

Al Saham

Apart from the dangerous wadis (rainwater gushing out from the mountains), the gush of water from about 150 kilometers to 93.206 miles from the mountains after the heavy rain, another serious hurdle for traveling between the interior towns was the dust storm of the desert—entire streets would be dark and the road to travel could not be seen. We would not be able to even cancel the fellowship meetings, as they would be waiting for us, and neither could we phone them up, as there were no cell phones those days. In the mornings, of course, there would be the fog, and sometimes serious car accidents would take place at such times.

We rented a small room in this town, which only cost about $23 per month. The rents were very cheap in Oman. About fifteen people could sit there. It had a door and an air conditioner. On occasion, twenty of us were able to manage. Only one Pakistani gentleman who worked in the hospital attended. Remaining were the nurses and the teachers. Doctors and officers normally did not attend these fellowships as they had cars and families to go to the distant mainline churches. Something unusual happened in this fellowship that we could never explain or sort out.

There was a nurse who cried bitterly one evening. She said that even before her marriage, a ghost would come to her bed and have fun with her. This continued after her marriage and after she was born again and after she had had children too. She could never get out of it. She would cry, weep, confess to Jesus, but whatever she did, the ghost never left her. Some of the senior nurses knew about this as she had shared it with them. We prayed for her in the group, and as we were praying, she fell down and got up, but there was no change in her life. The ghost continued to come.

At the same time, the Pakistani man shared a vision that *he saw a naked youth coming into the room* and walking all over the room and then disappearing. We had never shared with him about this particular lady's issue. This was a kind of coincidence; we did not know if this was connected to that lady's issue.

Finally, we decided to go to her house and pray, room by room. We started from the front room, and we began by praying for her first. She fell down again, but nothing happened; she got up after the prayer. We began to pray from room to room, sprinkling holy water, and as we went to her bedroom, it was locked from inside. She tried her best to open but it did not open. We assumed it must be her husband inside; who would not like us to see him. We had nothing much to do in their house. As we got down their house; which was on the first floor. We walked a few yards on the unpaved road; we saw her husband walking, pushing the bicycle. *So, that was not her husband locked up in that room.* We shared this with our Anglican Bishop, he told us serving communion in that house could help. We never met her again as, it was the summer break, we moved on.

The worship and devotion in that small room was great. I enjoyed. My heart and soul felt the worship there. I had also just given up my lucrative job to serve the Lord voluntarily, while we were singing the hymn Old Rugged Cross." Tears just rolled down my cheeks as I had surrendered everything to God and I did not have anything more to surrender to Him. All to Jesus. I surrender all to Him. I give.

This fellowship was held from 3:00 p.m. to 5:00 p.m. on Thursdays, and from there we moved back to Kaburah at 5:30 p.m., and from Kaburah we would get something to eat and then move on to Bideya at 10:00 p.m.

There was another interesting conversation going on between a Christian and a Sudani (Muslim) teacher in a teachers' hostel. They always read the Daily Bread before going to sleep in the night. Many questions were asked by the Muslim teacher to the Christian teacher. The teacher would get back to me and discuss the questions asked by the Sudani teacher. Sometimes I would help the teacher in giving her the answers.

One of the comments made by the Sudani teacher was that she liked all about Jesus but not what He said about turning the other cheek when one cheek is slapped. She said she wouldn't be a coward, as Jesus would put it.

"But I tell you not to resist an evil person. But whoever slaps you on your right cheek, turn the other to him also" (Matt. 5:39 NKJV). The answer given to that was Romans 12:19 (KJV), "Dearly beloved, avenge not yourselves, but rather give place unto wrath: for it is written, *Vengeance is mine; I will repay, saith the LORD.*"

"God is jealous, and; the Lord revengeth, and is furious; the Lord will take vengeance on his adversaries, and he reserveth wrath for his enemies" (Nah. 1:2 KJV).

She then understood the depth of the vengeance if God had to take it upon Himself. She was extremely happy about God taking vengeance.

Al Sohar

The American hospital in sun-drenched Muttrah was where Dr. Wells Thoms served as a physician for thirty-one years, treating contagious, fatal diseases until his retirement in 1970. Since then, stories of the noble, selfless man have been passed down through generations of Omanis. Starting with a team of only five Omanis, Thoms treated patients in roofless wards under the baking heat, not only in Muttrah, where he lived, but also as far as Barka and Sohar, before roads were built.

Sohar was famous because of its copper mine. We had been to see the deep huge pit dug for copper. The town site is located approximately 24 kilometers / 14.913 miles north of the coastal town of Sohar. The housing within the town site consists of a variety of accommodations, artistically furnished and centrally air-conditioned. The township has all basic amenities and facilities.

Oman Mining Company LLC (OMCO) is a state-owned company established by a royal decree based in Sohar, north eastern Oman. Its core activities are resource development and production of various minerals and aggregate inclusive of copper, gold/silver, chromite, lime, and silica till 1994. From the last quarter of 1994, owing to depletion of ore bodies in and around Sohar, copper production from indigenous ore has been discontinued (Oman Mining Company LLC).

Sohar was a place where the Nestorian Christians lived. A Nestorian bishop was seated there. In AD 325, the First Council of Nicaea was declared and formed the Nicene Creed. About 525 bishops went to Turkey to sign the Nicene Creed. The Sohar bishop was one of the 525 bishops who signed and declared the Nicene Creed (Wikipedia). Thereafter, there was no church building and priest; it was Ernest who was ordained and commissioned as an Anglican priest there. The first pastor after many centuries. There was another Pentecost pastor who had a Pentecostal group in Sohar for several years before Ernest.

To begin with, the fellowship was started in the town of Sohar on the coast. There were Sri Lankans and Indian teachers and nurses attending. We got connected to some

Filipino workers in an Oman copper mine. There was a Filipino Christian high official working in the copper mine. They were all excited about the fellowship in Sohar, and they invited us to meet in the copper mine township called Magan. They gave us a big hall and sometimes good dinner from the restaurant of the copper mine. The general manager of the company was a South Korean, and his wife was a believer in the Lord. She also started attending the fellowship. The keyboard player was also a Filipino. In this group we had British, Filipinos, Pakistanis, Indians, and Sri Lankans. The group was quite an interesting group and was multiethnic.

The fellowship went on very well for some time. Slowly, tests of our faith crept in. The South Korean general manager's wife had issues with her breast; she knew for sure that it was breast cancer, for that was their family hereditary issue, so they left. She was a source of encouragement to us. Once, I had asked her if she would underline the important verse in the Bible. She said every word in the Bible is important, so which verse to underline? I was very much impressed by that and I remember that even to date. It so happened after several years, when Ernest visited South Korea, he took her old phone number given to us before they left Oman. He just said he would call her and find out how she was. To our sorrow, she had already fallen asleep in the Lord. How I wish to see her in heaven. My Lord has prepared a room for all of us to rest in His glory. What a hope!

The Filipino manger had some issues too. He had fever that never left him, and they could not find out what was wrong with him. So he left Oman and went back to the Philippines, where they diagnosed some kind of bug in his lugs contracted in another country where he was working before. It was difficult to find a suitable medicine for that infection. We depended on God for healing, and the Lord did heal him. Praise God!

There was a teacher from Sri Lanka. We did not understand what she was saying. She was a Buddhist and came to know the Lord personally. She knew that Jesus was born to a virgin. She would always say she was also a virgin, like Mary, when her daughter was born. But we never asked why she was saying it like that. That was too personal, we thought. One day, she said in the middle of the night somebody came to her room with black dress and pulled her leg out one by one. The next day, she had a very upset stomach. Like before, we suggested that she should always play worship songs in her room and keep reading Scripture. She was all right after that, never complained.

The leader of the Sohar fellowship had a discussion with me over a particular issue about one of the members in the fellowship. All the while, I knew my thoughts were right, but God taught me not to tell that I was right and to humble myself before the leader and tell her what I wanted to say in a humble way. She perhaps did have the feeling that she won the argument, but that was okay with me. If she was happy, I was happy too. This lesson still carries me through.

We heard the king of the country always went on rounds at 2:00 a.m. He would personally get all the information of the people on their lifestyle. He would look into their needs and would meet them. On a beautiful, sunny day, he met some Christian leaders and asked them if they needed a church in Sohar. If they did, they should get the signature of some

Christians requesting for a place to worship the Lord. As a result, a huge land was given to the Christians, half of it for Catholics, and the remaining half for the Protestants. The Catholics built their church much earlier than the Protestants did.

All the denominations joined together and built a church. There were nine leaders chosen for that purpose. The bishop of the Middle East and Cyprus diocese and the Christians from Iran and Kuwait came to dedicate the church building after it was built.

We have heard the saying which says, "Too many cooks spoil the broth." There was always confusion, and it was not easy to get agreeable conclusions with nine board members operating the church administration. As a result, the main Anglican Church in the capital was responsible for the discipline of any church premises given by the government. Therefore, they decided on three officials to control and make decisions, with Ernest being the chairman, the leader of the Pentecostal churches as the secretary, and a doctor from Marthoma church as treasurer. They had great understanding and respect for one another. Things went on smoothly after that.

The Sohar-Magan fellowship, which met in the copper mine, had to move into the church building. Since there was no church, we had met as a house fellowship. Now that a church building was given by the king generously, we chose to meet there. The unfortunate thing that happened to us was, there was a Marthoma gentleman in the fellowship who was the treasurer of the fellowship, left us to join the Marthoma church. The person who helped us in bringing the people to the fellowship also started a Tamil church in the church building, as he was Tamilian. The Filipinos started their own English congregation. Very few of us were left behind. That was a heartbreaking issue. In any case, an Anglican church was started.

We had three worship leaders; one worked with Toyota, another worked in the Sohar hospital, and the third one worked with the construction workers. The construction worker had some issues with his pending salary. Since he was working with the migrant labor workers, he was very familiar with all the migrant labor camps. He was a very spiritual person and also knew the Word of God well. It became easy for us to use him to build up the migrant labor work. It was easy for him to communicate with them as well, as he knew three of their mother tongues well.

We encouraged him and used him to build up four congregations in four different languages, namely Malayalam, Urdu, Tamil, and Telegu. We had a Pakistani gentleman to be the leader of the Urdu congregation, a Tamil gentleman to be the leader of the Tamil congregation, and for the Telugu, a Telugu-speaking young guy as leader. These four congregations met in four different rooms of the church building, and after the service was over, they would all come to the main hall for Communion and Ernest would celebrate the Communion. When the Urdu fellowship met, I could hear all their prayers from outside. They were mostly from Pakistan; their leader was also from Pakistan. Some of them had not been paid for quite some time. To hear their prayer asking God to give them food was most heartbreaking. The English congregation also met at the same time in the main hall, and Ernest conducted it. The congregation grew well and was immensely blessed by the Lord.

At this time, Ernest also applied for two other vehicles. Since the work grew in leaps and bounds, Ernest applied to the owner of the top Omani gentleman to give the vehicles on discounted rates. He generously approved, in spite of knowing these vehicles were used for Christian activities. One we used, and the other one was used by the leader of the immigrant labor work.

The third vehicle was given to another couple like us who was also interested in the same work as we did in the interior part and the mountains of Oman. They were much younger than us and would handle the mountains well. We also went along with them. Ernest would preach the gospel, and they would support us in prayer and driving. I always called this particular friend of ours "the king of the mountains," as he would easily find the routes in mountains. If we left him at one end of the Hijar range of mountains, he would safely drive to the other end.

A set of migrant labor workers and some families were meeting for all-night prayers on alternate Saturdays. Every individual, on their turn to pray, prayed for us. The power of prayer for us was immense. Sometimes I would ask them to pray for other key matters instead of everybody praying for us. Still, they would not listen to me. They had to pray for us. Of course, that was our key for strength in the Holy Spirit. We praise God for this kind of fellowship that we enjoyed. At three in the morning, we would close the all-night prayer with a cup of coffee, then go home, sleep a little bit, and get ready for the morning church service. After the morning service, Ernest and I would go to Shinas for the fellowship with the Shinas group. When we got back at 3:00 p.m., delicious lunch would be waiting for us. Our migrant labor deacon would keep it ready for us. What a blessing that was!

On a Sunday morning, all the fellowship members visited the house of one of our friends. We had to climb up some steps to enter into their drawing room. There was another couple from our hometown in India, and they had a very bad news from India, that their house caught fire on December 23, 1992, and their young daughter withstood the fire and called the firefighters to do the needful. *The bold attempt that she made in sorting out the problem was suitably nominated for the Child Bravery Award for 1992* but was not selected by the government of India.

When we heard that their house caught fire and their daughter was managing the issue all by herself, we were concerned. Being concerned, I got out of our friend's house and started getting down their steps. These steps were very steep and huge, but my mind was full of the little girl, and the fear of fire that she had to face with her younger brother all by herself overtook me. *I tripped and rolled down the steps,* fell on the ground, hitting my head. My neck was hurt. I thought I was gone, but I was still there. All those who were inside the house came running, took care of me, got some ice, and helped me out. My neck was okay too. The most enjoyable fact was that Ernest took care of me very well. Perhaps I didn't mind falling again.

As I wrote this, I called the girl, who is now a lady, and asked about the details and told her I rolled down the steps when I heard that. Her reply encouraged me and moved me emotionally. She said, "It is really good to hear it because I truly felt no one cared about me during that time and I struggled with those feelings of abandonment for many years. Really feels like a balm on my spirit to hear it affected you so much because you cared."

Al Liwa

We had a fellowship in Liwa, though we went only once a month there. All were Sri Lankans, and we met in a Sri Lankan family's house. Except the host family, others attended one or two other fellowships. The couple was employed as teachers by the Ministry of Education. We mainly made it a point to attend this host and his family just to encourage them. They had a young son who was looking for a job, and God answered by giving him a job in the capital of Oman. Far away from where their parents lived. We were sometimes embraced by their great hospitality, providing us with grand dinner.

Al Shinas

Most of the members in this fellowship were men. There were three families attending other than some single men. It was a great fellowship. They were highly pleased that we went to meet them once a week, whether there was fog or dust storm on the road, and had a great time of worship and preaching time. They were immensely grateful as they would say that none of the pastors came to visit them. It was only Ernest. They worshipped in Malayalm, which was their mother tongue. They were great in singing worship songs. Even Ernest picked up the language and was worshipping in Malayalam along with them.

They were not a rich community. Most of them had small businesses, and also some had their own business but under an Omani head. Those who were in the habit of drinking alcohol gave up drinking after they accepted the Lord as their personal Savior. They were ever grateful to Ernest for going to pray with them and fellowshipping with them, whatever the hurdle might be.

None could really run a business in their personal names, though they owned the business. It was only the locals who were allowed to own "nameplates" of the business in their names, and the expatriates who owned the business were also to give a certain amount of money to the local Omani sponsor, who probably issued a visa for them to stay in Oman legally. For the Christian pastors, the king would give the visa through the nomination of the mainline churches.

There were two children of the host of the Shinas fellowship. They were in their schools. Both of them were very loving siblings. One would not stay without the other. There were other two children from two other families. While Ernest engaged the Bible study and worship for the elders, I would go to another room to take Sunday school for the children. On a fine day, I heard from the mother of the three-year-old girl that the little girl told her mother I was not teaching the Bible story in Malayalam for her to understand. This particular language, though a South Indian language, was not my mother tongue.

Well, I thought that was a first great complaint on me by a three-year-old girl. I should have known better. I had a smile on my face to myself!

I normally requested the older boy or his sister to interpret the story for her, but I think this cute little girl did not understand why I did not speak her language. This little girl would always come up with some interesting answers, in Malayalam, whenever I asked a question in English. She was great. After the class, the children would be asked to pray. All would pray, inclusive of the little girl. She would go on and on without stopping. I would think maybe she was praying in some language that I did not know. Finally, one day I asked them in which language she was praying. The boy, who was little older than her, said, "She is praying in English because you do not know Malayalam." I was amazed—she was just jabbering some syllables! Cute.

These children are now grown-up. After we left Oman, we heard the mother of the grown-up children had fallen asleep in the Lord. The older boy now is a doctor in Germany, and the girl is now married, with child. She is a dentist settled in India. I have no touch with the two younger ones. The amazing thing that happened in this fellowship was, the members who got connected to God again gave up their addiction for drinks. They were blessed. Praise God!

Al Nakhal

Reverend James Cantine, DD (March 3, 1861–July 1, 1940), was an American missionary, scholar, and traveler. His wife, Elizabeth, was a nurse and the first single woman to become a missionary in Arabia. Together they founded a women's clinic in Muscat, Oman.

It is said that Reverend Cantine had a house in Nakhal (the Golden Milestone). Nakhal is not on the coast, but they do enjoy the spring waters and falajas for their agriculture. It is a great place to visit with family and friends. It is a beautiful gift of God. Children can play in the spring water as it runs down the mountain. The water level is only knee-deep. The sand-colored walls of Nakhal Fort are surrounded by green palm trees that are fed by local irrigation systems called falajes that flow from the mountain springs above. Trickling down into the town are the Nakhal hot springs too, a place for locals and visitors to bathe and clean in the warm water.

The house church of Nakhal was only of Catholics. Except us two, all the others were Catholics. The host of the house was a doctor. He is also a great singer. He has sung some classics with celebrities. His wife was highly pleased to have prayer in their house. She was a very devoted person. Two great, oblivious miracles that happened were, the doctor who was an all-time addict for drinks gave up drinks overnight after attending the fellowship.

While the fellowship was going on, the host's sister-in-law visited the fellowship and told that she had colon cancer and needed prayer. After a week's time, she came back to the fellowship and said the Lord had healed her and she was cancer-free. *That was an amazing miracle of God! But she exhibited gratitude and faithfulness to Ernest by bowing to him in humility and surrender, with a beautiful gift in hand.* We were taken aback and were very much humbled. I heard, even till today, the

Lord has given her life. The Lord is our life giver. I am not sure how the other members of this fellowship are, but our host family is doing very well; the Lord's blessing to the family is multifold. We praise the Lord. Before I wrote this, I did ask my hostess friend what was the miracle the Lord did while we were fellowshipping with them. Immediately she said about the colon cancer of her sister-in-law, who is enjoying her health even till today.

Al Rustaq

Rustaq is also not on the coast, but they do enjoy the spring waters and falajas for their agriculture. As a city, it has maintained its old-world charm. Once the capital of Oman, it is full of historically significant structures. Located in the western side of the Hajjar Mountains, it is a city with farms fed by constantly flowing falaj. (It is said that it is the irrigation system from Solomon's time.) The hot spring is in the middle of the city. People from far and wide come to Rustaq for the healing quality of Ain al Kasfa. Its waters run at forty-five degrees Celsius (113 degrees Fahrenheit) and are regarded as a cure for rheumatism and skin diseases due to its sulfur content. The hot spring is said to have healing benefits, and although it is forbidden to swim at the main source of the spring, bathing areas are provided so people can enjoy its water.

Rustaq is famous for two important landmarks: Al Hazm Castle and Al Rustaq Fort. Al Hazm Castle is at the outskirts of Al Rustaq and is one of the most famous castles in the sultanate. The castle was built by Imam Sultan bin Saif II in the early eighteenth century, and he is buried in this castle along with his son. Al Hazm Castle features a beautiful wooden door with intricate writing. The fort is cradled by four tall towers.

We had good friends in Rustaq Hospital. We visited them along with our friends from the capital even while Ernest was an engineer. The senior couple there gathered all the Christians, and they were already meeting for prayer in the hospital. Our visit was a great encouragement to them. There was a good Sunday school running with the young couple who helped us in the mountain ministry.

Going to Rustaq was a great feast for us. The elderly couple looked after us with a lot of love and care. They fed us nicely—in fact, about seven rounds for a meal. There were two other elderly couple in that group, but they joined the place a little later. The youngsters were excellent in singing and worshipping the Lord.

The first mentioned seniors were the leaders. They organized all the fellowship meetings. Dinner was a part of every meeting. The gentleman was a singer and dancer. He always directed the choir. He limped a little bit while walking, but in spite of that, he would dance on occasions with some music and a smile on his face, which was a great delight.

The other senior gentleman was very well educated. He was married in the family circle to a nice, wise lady. Once, we, the friends who visited the interior even while Ernest was an engineer, had a gathering of a kind of retreat in Thermeid. The Lord used Ernest to witness to him after the sermon was over. He was fully convicted and had a sense of regret and guilt for losing all his fifty years of life not knowing the Lord and not serving Him. Soon after he was born again, he wanted to preach to the whole world about the Lord and was not willing to waste even a single moment of time. Hence, we encouraged him to take Bible studies in Thermeid and in Rustaq.

Another elderly couple was very hospitable. They had an organ in their house, and the lady played very well. Several times we had service in their house. The gentleman was the hospital engineer. He was a very nice, God-fearing gentleman. He fell very sick, and they did not make a fuss over it. They took it very well, in the strength of the Lord, and went back to India. The gentleman sweetly committed his life to the Lord and passed on to glory. The lady continues to serve the Lord and is full of His peace.

A doctor who attended the Rustaq church was passing by our Barka house once. He stopped at our house in the mid-afternoon. I am not sure why he stopped by our house. Normally, in Indian culture, when people visit us, we will not send them off without serving lunch or dinner. That particular day, Ernest and I were fasting and we had nothing cooked in the house. I mentioned that to him, but I volunteered to cook something and give it to him, which he refused. So many questions arise in my mind as I write this now.

Why did he come to our house at that part of the afternoon? What was in his mind? Did he need some help? Why did he go to the capital? What happened there? Did he go there for a medical checkup? No answers asking all these questions after many years. Was he hungry? But he gave me clear instructions not to bother about the food. Ernest prayed with him before he left. Did he just come for prayer? Soon after he reached home, he had a cerebral hemorrhage and was immediately admitted in the hospital in the capital. The mystery was, he had left a bunch of keys in our house. We handed it over to the people concerned. *Nobody knew about the mystery of the keys.* Not sure if the mystery is sorted out by now.

I can never forget one particular sister. She was teaching in a nursing college in Rustaq. She was a key member in the church. She resigned from her job and went to India.

We went to her hometown, where Vellore Christian Medical College is. Ernest was admitted there for his prostate gland issue. She came to know that I had had a big problem of leg pain since I was twelve years old. She advised me to get treated there and know what was really wrong with my legs, as there was a very good rheumatologist there. I was not very happy to do that, for my concentration was on Ernest. After advising me several times, slowly she took me to the registration counter and paid full money for my investigations. Though we gave back the money to her, I was humbled by her generosity and love. Praise the Lord! We have people around us to prove that they are the followers of the commandment of Jesus to love one another as He has loved us. Amen.

Many people left Rustaq. I am writing this after seventeen years of being there. I wish I could visit that place again and check what is happening, if the church is still being conducted there. Jesus said, *"If you do not praise Me, the rocks will."*

Qurayyat

Qurayyat is a small fishing town eighty-three kilometers southeast of Muscat, Oman, adjacent to the towns of Sur. There was a Sri Lankan doctor's family there. Our Sri Lankan friends from Sohar wanted us to visit them. We went there once a month for two months and prayed with them. The lady of the house had a lot confusion and ill feeling about the housemaid. She did not know if they were correct, and she wanted me to advise her on that. I did advise her to pray about it. God wants us to honor our feelings in the light of His wisdom and then prayerfully decide. Especially, we Indian women go by the wind and alter or adjust our life situations as per the blow of the wind. This lesson was a great lesson for me as well. This happened many years back, but even till today, I just think of it and *bring the feelings of mine to the throne of grace and ask Him to sort out the issues for me.*

Al Wadi Mistal Hospital

Wadi Mistal is part of the wadi collection on the Nakhal–Al Rustaq road. The main attraction is the green Wukan village situated at the end of the path, a nice place where tourists can see amazing gardens irrigated by an intriguing falaj system carefully maintained by the few existing locals. Wadi Mistal leads through a narrow gap in the mountains to an enormous desert basin. Dotted with acacia and grazed by goats, this basin is bisected by a good paved road that offers spectacular mountain views along its entire length. These wadis are mountainous areas where rainwater, when it rained, gushes out and runs about 200 or 250 miles. They run into towns and villages. It is quite dangerous as they run without prior notice.

There is a history that said while one of the sultans of Oman was taking some slaves in the wadi, the rainwater gushed into the road. In order to save the slaves, he jumped into the waters and was also killed. As I read this, it reminded me very much of our Lord Jesus; in order to save us, He gave Himself for us on the cross.

In our days there, there were no paved ways. We had to go on four-wheel drives while we climbed up and down the mountains. Now, the routes of some of these wadis are beautifully laid in asphalt. It is lovely to drive across. If you can click on wadis of Oman, you would find beautiful, enjoyable ones.

To visit the wadi hospitals and meet with the staff for prayer, we had to take permission from the head of the nurses in the main office. We went along with some of our friends to Wadi Mistal. Normally, we visited the staff of the hospital and had Bible study and prayer with them. They were great singers. We always enjoyed their worship and singing. He was able to interpret the sermons preached in their mother tongue to English. This particular time we went, I wanted to go into the hospital and have a look at all the patients. When we went around, we happened to come across an eighty-year-old local lady who had broken her spinal cord and so was admitted in the hospital forever.

We went near her. I could not talk to her, but I did pray, asking the Lord to be with her, and also, I expressed my desire to the Lord, saying, *"Lord, please let me see her in heaven."* I came back home, rolled on my couch, and all that happed, all that we did and said in the wadi hospital, also rolled over in my mind. I thought of the prayer I had prayed, "Lord, let me see her in heaven." By this prayer I did not twist the hand of the Lord and did not insist that He should answer my prayer. I thought I was praying according to His will. "None should perish". "For God so love the world, that he gave His only begotten Son that whosoever believes in Him should not perish but have eternal life." And then again, I thought of another verse, John 14:14 (KJV), *"If ye shall ask any thing in my name, I will do it." I was also told that "In my name" means "In His will."*

I was quiet but thinking. How would God answer my prayer? Who would tell her the plan of salvation, in Arabic? I was not even sure that she could speak; she was very silent when we saw her. We were only told that her family had left her there for the medical care. She was cuddled and appeared like a tiny girl, thin and skinny, facing toward the wall. Suddenly, it dawned on me very quietly. *In silence I heard the Lord speaking that He has no language barrier; He understands and he can speak all languages. He need not utter words as we do to verbalize what He has to say. He can communicate through the wind, the storm, the rain, the thunder, the lightning, or through the nurse while administering medicine or through the sway of the curtain. He could come to her in a vision or a dream. She could see a cross with Jesus on it. She could see the blood oozing from Him and think of the sacrifice of the sheep or lamb or of any animal on Eid days. For the forgiveness of the sins, right? Do I believe that I will see her in heaven? Yes, I do.* The Lord considers us as His co-laborers. And His commission to us is, "And he said unto them, go ye into all the world, and preach the gospel to every creature" (Mark 16:15 KJV).

Another breathtaking thing that happened was in our visit to another wadi hospital, Wadi Bani Ghafir. Normally, visitors are not allowed to visit the patients, but the locals do appreciate and respect the priests, so it was easy for us to get into the hospital after the prayer. When we went around, there was a blind and deaf local guy. We decided to pray for him. One of our friends prayed for him. We prayed in English—perhaps he did know English. *Being a deaf and blind man, he couldn't see either, but when we said "Amen," he also said "Amen." That was amazing!* We were extremely happy. The only possibility of him saying "Amen" would be that his spirit must have gotten in touch with the Holy Spirit while praying.

Wadi Hibi

Wadi Hibi is located about eighty kilometers (sixty-five miles) from Sohar and meanders between rugged mountains and date palms. Its main attractions are the fort, which has two large courtyards, as well as its many natural water pools, between the rugged mountains and date palms. We knew a director of nursing working in the Sur area in Oman. She was the one who had to issue permission to enter into the hospital accommodation. Since she was from our hometown, it was easy for us to obtain permission all over the interior of Oman from the Sur side. She helped us to meet the staff workers of the hospital in Ibri, Izki, Nizwa Ibra, and Sur. Our friends the young couple were mainly in charge of these places. Ernest, their mentor and friend also went along with them. I did go sometimes.

We visited Wadi Hibi with our senior pastor from the Reformed Church of America. Along with us were two inspectors of schools for the teachers who taught English as a second language, and their spouses. Some hospital staff members and many others were present that day. We had the

Bible study and the prayer in the house of an elderly gentleman. He had an issue; he said every morning his dead mother would call his name into his ears and wake him up from sleep. He also said he always had a feeling of crashing his car against another car coming across him. We prayed for him. And then we had no time to discuss with him further; we had to move on to a health center there and celebrate the Communion in a lonely health center in the desert. We rejoice over this celebration, *perhaps that was the first time in the middle of the desert that the Lord's supper was celebrated.*

We were deeply emotional. We praised God all along the way. We virtually sprinkled the blood of Jesus, praying for God to let all those who tread on that path come to the salvation experience of the living Lord Jesus Christ. Even from today and forever. Till the world ends into a new earth and new heaven. The prayers we said will echo all over Oman. Praise the Lord!

Al Ain

Al Ain literally means "spring." It is a city in the eastern region of the Emirate of Abu Dhabi on the United Arab Emirates border with Oman, adjacent to the town of Al-Burami. Al-Ain is known as the Garden City of Abu Dhabi, the UAE, or the Gulf, due to its greenery, particularly with regard to the city's oases, parks, tree-lined avenues, and decorative roundabouts.

There was a youth pastor in Al Ain who somehow got some information on us and approached us, asking us to visit Al Ain and pray for a girl who was possessed. Like great warriors, in all boldness showered by the Lord Jesus Christ, we went. Our deacon was with us; he was great in driving on new roads. This girl worked in a hospital, and her hospital accommodation was also very well furnished. This girl perhaps was in her twenties, very beautiful and very well dressed. Looked like some celebrity. Her hair and nails were all in beautiful colors. We were asked to pray for her, to be set free. We started singing worship songs. Ernest is a great singer when there is nobody to listen. Funny, right?

As we started singing, she fell from the chair onto the floor. Her hair came out, and she started hitting her fist against the floor. She would now and then look at us with fearful eyes. She kept on hitting the floor till she got up peacefully from the floor onto the chair. She never ever complained about the pain on her wrist or fist, which was used to hit the ground several times. I am sure I can't even hit the ground with my wrist even once without feeling the pain of it.

She narrated the entire ancestral story of being possessed. The main thing that was told to us was that as she entered her apartment from work, she would see all the dead old men with long beards sitting in her room. There was a big story to back it up. I restrain from writing about this, lest my readers may not be able to face the fear of it. We gave her the gospel and asked her to attend a suitable Bible-believing church.

My Parents onto the Arms of Jesus

As my father grew older, he developed Alzheimer's disease; it was quite difficult for my brother, who was in charge of him, to look after my father, as he would go away wherever. So, they had to lock the gate and keep him inside or take him out by themselves. He would always talk about the mission hospital that he worked at and the house that they gave for him to live. That was the only topic he would talk about to all the people who came to see him. My mother was highly diabetic and had suffered from stomach ulcers all her life. For some strange reason, which she told me alone, she couldn't attend to her ulcers while she was young enough to do so for the doctor was my father's boss. There was another government hospital in the town. Nobody would go to the government hospital, having the mission hospital on hand.

Every year during summer vacations, we would go see our parents and spend time with them. It so happened that when we went to see her in 1994, our flight to Muscat was canceled and we had to go back to our house. Laying my head on my mother's lap, I did get an opportunity to talk to my mother about Jesus again. She knew the Lord and was quite meticulous in praying, having family prayers and seeing that we grew in the knowledge of the Lord. But she would never say she had accepted the Lord as her Savior. She had a lot of bitterness toward her mother-in-law, who ill-treated her, and her older brother, who treated her badly. So, *I did speak to her about forgiving and forgetting the hurts they had caused her.*

That was the last conversation I had with her. Summer of 1995, we had to go to the US. I did take her permission if it was okay for her if we did not see her that summer. She consented. As I think of it now, I grieve. Days do not get back. What we leave behind are left behind, and we may never be able to pick them up. That is why perhaps the proverb goes, "Opportunity strikes only once."

Somehow within myself, I had a strong feeling that I should be writing to her more about heaven and what would happen to those who believe in the Lord Jesus after death. I mentioned this to her in all my letters in many different mild ways. *She had kept my letters under her pillow.*

I got back to work, and I had a strong urge to talk to my mother. Those days I could not make calls from home. We did not have international connections. We had to talk to our parents from the booth with cards. We had a booth in the petrol station, so we would call our parents from there. I did not have a card to talk to her, though I had a strong urge to call her. The school work that day was also very heavy. I said to myself that I would call her the next day. The next day never came. I went to bed that night, but early in the morning, at four o'clock, our land phone was ringing. It was from our hometown. My brother was calling to say our mother was no more; she had a massive heart attack. I could not forgive myself. If only I had called her, in obedience to my urge, and said goodbye.

Her final words to me were, "Please tell Lali [that is me] I have been saved."

After my mother died, it was very difficult for my father to live. He would crawl on the bed and plead to God. Even on her deathbed, he would not understand the concept of her death. He would sit next to the coffin and tell us that if we took her to the mission hospital, got surgery done, she would be all right.

Well, I had to leave him too. Life goes on and should go on. When I bade farewell to my father, he asked me not to go. He said I should work in the mission hospital and they would look after me well and would give me a house to live. I just told him I was going just for an outing and would be back. That never happened. The next day, when I called him, he could never recognize me.

After six months of my mother's death, I had the same urge that I had for my mother before she died to call home. This time I had the card to call, and a booth had been installed in the school where I worked. I had to walk about half a mile to get to the phone booth. The heat was 104 degrees Fahrenheit. I walked to the booth several times in the heat, for the phone would not work. The line was not going to India. But I did not give up. This time, I had to listen to the inner urge of calling home and talking to my brother who looked after my father. Well, after several calls made in perseverance, finally I got connected to my sister-in-law. The call did not last more than a minute. She told me that my father was admitted to the hospital as he could not eat anything. I called my doctor friend, and she told me that it could be connected to the brain, could be a brain hemorrhage.

I wanted to leave Oman immediately and go see my father. I've always believed that if a man is sick, either his wife or his daughter should be there to take care of him. I am not sure if the sons or the daughters-in-law would cuddle them as the wife or the daughter would. I had to go to the Ministry of Education office to get leave and my passport, which was submitted to the office while I took up the job. The ministry officials did not believe me when I told them the need of my travel. As I was teaching the final years, they recognized the importance of my presence. Moreover, that was the period of Ramadan, so they thought I was just taking a break. I was persistent; I would not leave the office till they let me go with my passport. I told them I was what I was because of my father. I was willing to resign from my job to go see him, in case they did not let me go. Finally, the school inspector had to come to my rescue and stood guarantee for my absence.

Well, we got back to India. I went straight to see my father. He lay there on the bed, pathetic indeed. I knew I had to get back. Only for six days, I was allowed to stay. I wanted to give my father all the best comfort I could give. He was eighty-six years old then. I could not ask God to heal him and give him a longer life. He lived well; he ran the race well. His family, wife, and children were the apple of his eyes. Though he told us many times he could not accept the Lord as his Savior because of the lies that he had to say, I did see him crawling on the bed and asking Jesus to help him out after my mother died. Though that sight was very hurting, still that satisfied me to know that he was connected to God.

He never recognized me when I went to see him. I could see him looking up to the sky now and then, and I wondered what he was seeing up there. Was it my mother, who had gone ahead of him, or were there some angels seen? No answer. Leaving him in that condition and getting back to Oman for work, keeping true to my word, was fearful for me. I went around requesting all the nurses to take care of him well. The doctors never visited frequently, and even if they did, they would not tell me what was happening with my father. It was on the fifth day of my being in India with my dad when, in the evening, my dad kept on looking up and was also looking at me several times. When I realized he was looking at me several times, I kept telling him, "Appa, I am Lali." (Dad, I am Lali.) He nodded and told me, "Ahh." My joy knew no bounds! I went around telling everyone that my dad recognized me. Praise God!

That evening, as I was sitting by the side of my dad's bed, my youngest brother, with whom my dad was living, came to the hospital. Both of us read the Bible to our father and then both prayed. Undoubtedly, God led us to pray, committing our father's spirit to the Lord, whom we loved. After this, we spent some more time with our dad and then left for home. That night, I did not sleep; just one day was left for me to leave India. I could not leave my dad in that situation and go to a foreign land. *I kept on praying, asking my Lord to do something. My only one-sentence prayer from the bottom of my heart, with agonizing in spirit, connecting myself to my heavenly Father,* was a request to

Him to do something. The intimacy of God the Holy Spirit and my spirit that night is indescribable.

Well, at 5:00 a.m., I got the news that my father had fallen asleep onto glory. The main sad thing was, I was not next to him while he went home. In all these I understood that life is nothing but a cycle of birth and death, and in the process, some who are saved by His grace will go to glory. What a hope that one day we will all be there, up above, with our most loved Jesus, who gave Himself for us on the cross of Calvary, exhibiting His great love.

My brothers brought the body of my dad home. That evening was the funeral service. We finished it, and straight away I left for the airport.

Our Dear Friend

Our friend was a very polite gentleman who cared for others. He was a man with genuine self-confidence. He knew his mind, and he was not afraid to stand up for what he believed. He was calm. He never spoke a word more than what he should speak. He was a very unassuming friend. He always spoke about the Bible whenever we met. He was an ardent worshipper of God. He was exposed to Christianity even while he was young. His father worked in a mission organization in India, and though they were Hindus, they respected Christianity a lot.

He lived in Musanna. He had a small car, which perhaps would not go more than four miles. He attended the Musanna fellowship, which was held at 10:00 p.m. He and his wife worked till 9:00 p.m. every day except on a Friday. He was a pharmacist in a private pharmacy, and she was a nurse in a private medical clinic. Their salaries were not that great, but they were content with what they got and what they had. They had two children who lived in their hometown in India. Since we were going to the Magan fellowship in Sohar on Fridays, he also wanted to go along with us. That gave both Ernest and this gentleman a great opportunity to discuss the Bible, and I was a silent listener.

Therefore, we picked him up from his house and dropped him back after the fellowship every Friday. Some days, on the way back, he would request us to go to his house so that he could have some extended time with us, and his wife would give us something to eat. On the wall, he had displayed the huge pictures of all the photos of all the Hindu gods, and also the photo of Jesus. It also proved his worship for them by the way he had decorated them with flowers and frankincense.

Days went by, and he began to learn more of Jesus and began to taste of His love. He slowly understood why Jesus was sent to the world by His Father God and why Jesus had to die on the cross, and the significance of Jesus's resurrection. He understood the concept of the plan of salvation as his gift from God.

The cause for Jesus's birth, death, and crucifixion, along with His resurrection, was clearly understood by him. He also understood the grace of God and the plan of salvation. He found a lot of peace in Jesus in his life, and the attitude toward his life changed considerably. In times of loneliness, it was Jesus who was their companion. After receiving Jesus as his Savior, he began to tell everybody about Jesus, and he also wanted to preach. Members in the Magan fellowship were not happy that he wanted to preach before getting baptized; according to them, he was still a Hindu.

We did not force him on that, in a subtle way, as we traveled to Sohar, keeping all the photos on his wall in mind; we would tell him that Jesus is a possessive God, a jealous God, and He said that there is no other God before Him.

"I am the Lord, and there is none else, there is no God beside me: I girded thee, though thou hast not known me: God is a jealous God" (Isa. 45:5 KJV). It is part of His nature.

"You shall not bow down to them or worship them; for I, the LORD your God, am a jealous God" (Exod. 20:5–6 ESV).

We never forced him or never pressurized him to believe on this. He would be silent; never said a word about this.

Perhaps the members of the Magan fellowship told him that he should not be preaching before he got baptized. On a particular Thursday morning, some Sri Lankan friends wanted to get baptized. Coming to know of this, he picked up a taxi and came fast to our house to go with Ernest to the baptismal place. Unfortunately, Ernest had already left. I had not gone that day with Ernest. I was at home. I was told that his wife got fed up of him for constantly telling her that he wanted to get baptized, so she threw some towels and told him, "You want to do it, go get it done."

The next Friday, we went to his house to pick him up for the Magan fellowship. When he got into our car, he was crying. We wondered why. Slowly he unfolded himself. The story goes like this. He had given his car to the workshop for servicing, and that got burnt there. All that he had in the car were also burnt.

That was a sad thing, indeed, but when we heard the news, we prayed with him. I also felt within myself that maybe this was happening to him because the Lord was teaching him something special, and also, I decided, on our return, we should go to his house to pray with the family. When we went to the Magan fellowship, during the fellowship time, he wanted to talk to the members and request them to pray for him. Amid his sobbing with tears and wiping his eyes, he told the brothers and sisters what happened to his car.

On our return, I suffered from a lot of inferiority complex. I wondered why we needed to go to his house. For what? Were we real, great, powerful people? If we prayed, would that be answered? So, on and so forth, all kinds of negative feelings about going to his house and praying. Nearing his house, he requested us several times to go to his house and have something to eat. Somehow, finally he had his way; we had to oblige. So, we went. To our amazement, as soon as we got into the house, we noticed all the photos of other gods were removed; only the photo of Jesus was there.

We sat on the couch in their house restfully after the day's heavy work, facing the photo of Jesus. We talked about various issues. Perhaps it helped him to forget his car a little bit. His wife served us something to eat, and as we were eating, there was a knock on the door. He opened it and saw the owner of the car servicing workshop, a Pakistani gentleman. He stood there with a car key! He said, "I burnt your car. I went to the secondhand-car yard and bought a car for you. Here is the key." What a God we serve! Amazing!

What a nice gentleman was the workshop man! When there was another set of people who wanted to get baptized, our friend and his wife both were there at that time, all set with towels to get baptized. They both went back to India and went from village to village in India to preach the gospel of Jesus. Oh! As I write this, how I wish to see them in heaven!

At the same time back in India, his mother, who was connected to some Christians, also got baptized. It was a miracle too! After a few days, his father, who was sitting on an easy chair, watching *The Pilgrim's Progress*, fell asleep in the Lord.

It's Us

Ernest was ordained as a priest. It was a little difficult for me to be a pastor's wife. There is a lot of difference between being an engineer's wife and a priest's wife. As an engineer's wife, I joked around a lot, pulling everybody's legs. Once, I was pulling all the ladies, asking them to kiss the bishop's ring as he entered. He yelled at me, "Lalitha, when you don't do it, why do you ask others to do it?"

The Bible society in charge, Mr. Longer Necker, once came along with us to the Magan fellowship to display the books. It was 10:00 p.m. by the time we left that place.

Our Bible society brother could not drive without feeling drowsy, and both of us were dozing. To avoid sleep, he went on talking and talking, but since we were drowsy, we could not concentrate on what he was saying. He just went on and on. He managed to drive down straight on the south, and as we came near our house, he had to make a circle around the roundabout and then on to left, but I was afraid in his sleep he might take a circle around the roundabout and then on to the right and go straight north again instead of south. When I warned him about it, he told me, "Oh, Lalitha, keep up your humor."

Just one day before the ordination of Ernest, we were to attend a retreat. The archbishop, intuitively knowing the seriousness of my fearfulness to be a priest's wife, did advise me to be just as I am. Nevertheless, I did become serious, no more joking or fooling, lest the congregation might not take me seriously, might not believe whatever I said; they would assume I was just joking. Since I am a very serious person within myself, sometimes I let out the steam inside me with some light, ethical jokes. I do not appreciate biblical jokes. Ernest, too, has some simple, casual talks and laughs aloud, and those who listen to him laugh will also laugh a lot; it will sound funny because he laughs.

We never told the people about us. We never told them about our education or about the position that we held, lest they would put us on some high pedestals. We never even told them about our birthdays or wedding anniversary. We did not want them to hero-worship us by boosting our ego, but rather focusing our attention toward the kingdom of God. All that they assumed about us was, "Here is a couple without children going from door to door, focusing on the Lord's kingdom."

I would be a single teacher to teach in Sunday schools in all the house fellowship. I would teach the children Bible in another room while Ernest was preaching to the parents. This was also to maintain silence in all the house fellowships. Some fellowships had musical instruments, and for some others, clapping hands were the rhythmic musical instruments. In a week, I would teach in seven Sunday schools, and also, I would be teaching full-time in the school for older girls. In addition to this, I would spend the nights worshipping God and interceding for those who needed prayers. Isn't it the Lord's strength and grace, passion, and enthusiasm given by Him?

Oman Anglican Church is a dual-chaplaincy church co-administered and celebrated by the Reformed Church of America and the Anglican Church. Ernest was ordained by the Anglican Church; as we were cradle Anglicans, there is a bit of difference in the method of service from India, the Arab Anglican churches, and the American Anglican churches, though the liturgy is the same.

In a nutshell, our work in Oman would be from May 1984 to July 2004. Ernest worked as an engineer in Oman for six years, after the call of God, on a full-time basis; for six years in the interior ministry, under the headship of the Ruwi main church; then the Interserve and Indian Evangelical Mission for six years. Finally, another eight years with the Reformed Church of America and Anglican Church in Ruwi. All in all, he worked in Oman for twenty years. I worked as a teacher with the Ministry of Education for thirteen years and then on had a school of our own for five years.

The American Reformed Church pastor who came as a pastor of our church in Ruwi to Oman took a lot of interest in the interior ministry that Ernest was doing. He also chose to work in the interior, just as Ernest did. The entire interior work was divided into three areas; three pastors were responsible for the northeast of Oman, the inland of Oman, and the coastal area. Inclusive of the wadis. As a result, the Reformed Church also gave salaries to all three pastors. That was the time when I resigned from the job and was supporting Ernest in the thesis that he had to do online with Fuller Seminary. Ernest by now was the full-pledged pastor of the newly built church in Sohar, along with the east coast house fellowships. The sweet couple who helped us in inland mission work also left to the United States for further studies. They have their own church in States now.

It was only one gentleman in the Rustaq fellowship who had something to say about my resignation. He was not happy that I had resigned from my job. He told me, "You like children a lot, and you may wish to give them some gift now and then. But if your pocket is empty, how will you do that?" I had no answer for him. In my mind I thought, Even otherwise, my pocket would be empty.

We met the bishop after that over a cup of coffee. I told him about my resignation, but he did not have a word to tell me. I also told him, "Bishop, now I feel I am a zero." But even to this, he was silent. Well, it might have been only once or twice I considered myself a zero, no more than that. The bishop must have prayed for me. I was always full of enthusiasm and full of vision for the Lord. I've heard that we need to have visions for the Lord; if we do not have a vision for the Lord, we perish. I have often asked the Lord, "God, why do You give me so many visions when I cannot achieve them for You?"

I consider myself as an encourager. Ernest would also tell me, "You encourage me and the Lord will encourage you." Yes, He does. God does encourage me. The gift of God for me is to encourage others. The Lord helps me to identify the talents in the individuals in the church and encourage them to take part in church activities. Christmas was very well celebrated in all the fellowships in islands northeast and southeast and wadis in Oman. All the members of the fellowships were invited, and the bosses, managers, and colleagues, who were mostly the locals. There would be a good nativity drama to explain why Christians celebrate Christmas and why Jesus was born to a virgin. Some fellowships had the costumes for the children's nativity show, and for about seven house fellowships, I would carry the costumes, with makeup. From fellowship to fellowship. Our vehicle was a mobile drama company. I would also dress up the children with the help of some parents.

Bait Namu Al Tafel

After my resignation from my work as a full-time teacher with the Ministry of Education, I spent time reading all about the history of Oman. I would help Ernest in his work in the mornings and then go with him in the evenings to the house fellowships to take Sunday school. After two years of staying at home this way, I was all in to get on to do some other adventure. My immediate passion was to start a school for the children below seven years who had nothing much to do. The school system began in Oman after seven years only. As a result of this passion, Ernest and I went several times to the capital of Oman, Muscat, to get the education ministry permission to start a nursery school. Nobody knew who can help us with the approval to obtain permission to go ahead and start a nursery school.

It was very tough to officially begin school. Moreover, in Oman, we were not supposed to get connected to the locals. Since I had lived there for fifteen years by then, and also since I had worked with Omanis in the school, I had picked up quite a bit of boldness to get things going. There were too many children below the age of seven all around the community where we lived. Therefore, to begin with, I had to rent a place.

The main church was most willing to give the rent, for they knew that I was a career woman and it might be difficult for me to sit at home.

I did find a house just two lanes behind our house. This was a house with three rooms, with no scope of further developing the building. Before starting school, we spent time in prayer for three days, during the morning hours. After three days, we did not know how to go about inviting the children to attend. No Omanis would believe if we were to tell them that we were starting the school. But we still went and sat in the building prayerfully. One day, as we were talking in our Indian language, the lady who lived behind that house heard us and came to see who these people were. She was a very friendly lady carrying a child, and another child around her walking, a little older than the baby she was carrying.

When she knew that we were starting a school there for small children, she was all excited. She said she would like to be a teacher and she would bring her nieces and nephews too. Finally, we thought God had answered our prayer. We extended our invitation for her to be a teacher as we also needed a teacher who could speak Arabic. There were some children next door to us too. We called them also. They came along with their older sister, who was in her twenties, and she wanted to be the teacher. So now I had two teachers and some children on hand.

The main church was also all excited about us starting a school, and they we were willing to give me whatever I wanted. Unlike the school I started in India, for which I shed a lot of tears to fulfill the passion, here I was delighted about how the

Lord was leading and providing all things that I needed. The families in Muscat, when their children grew up, would bring all kinds of toys to the church and leave it there for the needy parents. I would grab all those toys and bring them to school. I called myself a grabber.

We also visited the nursery school in Muscat meant for the rich children; they were also most willing to give us whatever we wanted. When we visited Pasadena Fuller Seminary, we met the wayfarers, and when they knew that I was running a school, they sent a lot of books and things that were required for children. With all those books, we made a small library for the children, and also, I could use all the biblical materials for the Sunday schools of the house churches. We bought all the colorful curtains, tables, and chairs, most modern ones. Making it look very colorful.

We had another Omani girl coming to the school, seeking a job. She also brought another Omani girl to the school for work. All these girls had finished thirteen years of schooling since the age of seven. They could not get admission to the Sultan Qaboos University because of their low grades and since the number of seats available in the university were just eighty since it was a new university. I welcomed all of them. Now we had four Arabic teachers who had just finished their secondary school and were sitting at home, not knowing what to do. They were not able to get married also.

As in Arab culture, especially that of Oman, the men had to give a certain amount of money to the bride if he had to marry her. Naturally, he would prefer to marry an educated girl with a good job. It was sad, indeed, to see these girls just sitting at home, without anything much to do.

An elderly Indian Pentecostal lady came to know through the church circle that we had started a school, so she also approached me for a job in the school. I welcomed her also. Now four plus one teachers apart from me!

The girl who was my neighbor had some issues. Her mother was very particular that I should take her to school. She was not even a secondary-school girl; she was just a few years of school-goer. She was an excellent worker at the school. Sometimes I had to pick her up every day at school. Without talking much, she would dedicate her time to work with the children and do all that she had to do meticulously. Praise God! She could not attend school because of epilepsy.

It was very risky to take her to school, but I didn't mind taking the risk. She often got it in the school, either at the beginning of the school, before the children came, or after all the children left. She had epilepsy in the school, but it did not happen while I or the children were there. A few days back, I heard she is now married, happy, and has her own family.

By this time, we also came to know that the lady inspectors of the child-care school, if at all she existed, was residing in the town of Sohar, where we had started school. Her office was also somewhere there. It was quite difficult to approach her; though I tried several times, she was never available, and even her office never gave me an appointment.

I believed that the children's span of attention was considerably less, so I adapted a system of working with the children in providing activities that they love for just fifteen minutes and kept changing activities once in fifteen minutes. It could be learning the alphabet, numbers, singing, or whatever; I would observe their desire to carry on with the same activity for a longer time, and then I would give them a little more time for the same activity. I believed that if the children were kept busy and if they loved what they were doing, the in-disciple problem would never exist. The alphabet was taught using all pictures and then to go with the alphabet song.

None of the teachers who came was teacher-trained. I was involved with research on teaching language through the communicative and communicational method of teaching English as a foreign language, so it was easy to follow the method in teaching English to the children and making them learn the language in a communicational way. Since I had also done some small action researches on the acquisition of English as a second language, it was discovered that a five-year-old kid can acquire five languages when exposed to them.

It became easier-to-follow steps in teaching English. While teaching in the college of education, I was also teaching the teacher trainees the different methodologies in teaching. But in this school now, there was no Montessori or kindergarten method; it was all my method.

I wrote some simple rhymes that made the Arab children learn English earlier. The first song they learned was, "What is your name?" the answer for which would be, "My name is Abdullah," and then Abdulla asking Mohamed, "What is your name?" "My name is Mohamed. Then it moved over to what someone's name was. "His name is Abdulla." Similarly, they would interchange to girls, "What is her name?" and to boys,

"What is his name?" They did not talk it out but sang it out. I had a tune for it, which made it sound like a nursery rhyme.

Later on, I moved to another grammatical usage on *have, has, had, I, you, we, they, do, does, done,* and *did,* which were all taught in songs. Showing them some objects and using the grammatical items in rhymes and learning to sing a song was easy for them; thereby, learning language and grammar was also easy for them. Taught the below with the help of the clock:

What is the time? The time now is twelve o'clock.
What is the time? The time now is eleven o'clock.
What is the time? The time now is ten o'clock.
What is the time? The time now is nine o'clock.
What is the time? The time now is eight o'clock.
What is the time? The time now is seven o'clock.
Ding dong, ding dong. Snore. (Acting out sleeping.)

Every sentence above had a different tone, so each child would enjoy the tone and the action that went along with the tone. Teachers and the children learned these songs while I taught. They were so very simple and easy for them to remember as well. I would demonstrate the songs with action for the first time when I introduced it. Then the teachers would pick up those songs and carry on with the kids.

As soon as the children came to the school, some would take up bicycles and some would play on the slides and other outdoor games. At 9:00 a.m., they would get in and watch some beautiful English cartoon videos. That would help them acquire some English language. Then for about fifteen minutes, they learned songs in English—I mean rhymes. For another fifteen minutes, some numbers and Arabic, and then some drawing and painting work. Once in fifteen minutes, they would change their activities and they were kept so busy they had no time for any mischief.

The great success in teaching is not in the methodology; it is the love for those to whom we teach. I did recognize all these young girls loved the kids. I could notice the great tribal bondage in them. Whenever they needed some kind of small suggestions or help, I was always there. I would also sit in the classes and observe their teaching. I could say that they knew that I loved them, and also the kids. Two strict rules they had to maintain: the first one is, they must never leave the kids alone, and they should never get on conversations, leaving the kids to mind themselves.

Though the teachers were the citizens of a rich country, they were humble and lovable. We paid for them very less. We collected less fees, and they were all from a lower middle class. I would distribute the fees to the teachers as their salary. They would be immensely happy about that because it was their pocket money for their sundry items. Even for the elderly Indian lady, it was great pocket money. She used to spend a lot of time with the Lord, praying for all of us. She loved what she was doing. She was not a teacher, but she was to maintain the cleanliness of the school, and also, she would clean up the children. Every morning at ten o'clock, we gave all the children Tang to drink and some cookies to eat.

One day, a mother brought three kids to the school, and all three kids were siblings. The first one was Mohammed and was ten years old but looked like a three-year-old kid. The second one was completely blind, a girl, and the third one was a boy, again half-blind. They were told this was a genetic issue because the parents were first cousins. They had taken the blind girl to all the hospitals and also all over India, but they were told she had no optic nerve. They could not do anything for the younger boy also, for he also did not have an optic nerve. The older boy, of course, would remain as a dwarf. He was very fond of playing ball with me. He would not tolerate it if I played ball with other kids. He appeared to be very possessive of me and would go to seclusion, being jealous.

There was a British in Oman, and he was a port consultant, working in Oman with the ministry. He was our church member in the Sohar church. His wife was a West Indies, a British, and equally as tall as he was—a handsome couple. She became my prayer partner. Having nothing to do in the house as a housemaker, she would come to school sometimes and enjoyed watching the children busily doing their activities. She was a great encourager to me and a strong supporter in all I did. She would also sometimes go with me to the shopping center in the evenings.

On the way, we would drive down to her house and share our issues and pray together. They left earlier than we did, so I missed my prayer partner forever. Well, she said the Lord would give me another one. I missed her a lot. What goes behind us may never get back.

There was another British professor at the university in Sohar, and he was coming to our church in Sohar. His wife and her friend visited Oman upon hearing about the school through the professor who wanted to visit the school. They were impressed. The advice that the lady gave me was that I should give one-tenth of the money I got from the school fee to the Lord, however small an amount it was. I appreciated that advice and was most willing to do that. But the church said I could keep it with me and use it for the school developmental work.

Once in Pasadena, we had gone to Fuller Seminary; there the neighbors of our apartment, knowing that I am from the Middle East, asked me to give a talk of the women in Islam. After the talk, the leader of the women's fellowship came to our apartment and gave me the leftover money of the meeting in a cover. I opened it and saw it; it was all in pennies. I was slightly hurt about it. I was not earning and did not look for money, but when I got the pennies, I asked God, "Is it all I am worth?" That was on a Saturday evening, so the next Sunday morning, when I went to church, I put the cover into the offering bag.

That was very special to me; though they were pennies, to have put the entire amount gave me an exuberant joy. Perhaps the women who put three coins to the offering must have felt the same way. After two days, the next-door neighbor brought a cover and gave it to me. It had two hundred dollars in it.

There was another local teacher, a young Omani girl who had just finished her studies. She was married. She always talked to me, saying she was a misfit to adopt her culture. She felt it was unfair for the wives to be at home while the husbands had their freedom. They would come home late in the night after their socializing with other Omani guys in the restaurants with delicious food. She would ask me why it was so. When both husband and wife earned the same but one had a better way of life, whereas the other did not. I would tell her life is an adjustment through Christ, in whom we find full freedom. I explained to her all about salvation. She would again get back to me and share her thoughts with me. But never to listen about Christ; she would tell me not to tell her about Christ, for she would say death would be an outcome if she listened to it.

We had a blow—all for good, I suppose. The owner of the school wanted us to leave the house. Maybe he was afraid, for we did not have a signboard. I was not sure of that, anyway. We started looking for another, and it did not take much time to find a bigger one. The owner was extremely happy to rent it out to us—just the opposite of the other owner. I was very happy about this building because we could extend the building on the west side and the north side. We built on the north side a huge shade for children to cycle and play outdoor games early in the mornings, as the temperature would be about 103 degrees Fahrenheit in the afternoon. We built a strong permanent shelter on the west side for the children to watch cartoons as if they were in a movie theater. And also to play indoors. The owner of the building was very happy about this. I now cannot remember how I got the money for that. God met the need.

Every morning, ever since the inception of the school, Ernest and I were praying for these children and the teachers. It was neither a coincidence nor an accident that one bright, sunny day, the TV in the school gave up. So, I did not know how best to engage the kids. I requested the teachers to tell them a story. One of the teachers agreed to tell the story in Arabic as she was fluent in Arabic, and the kids would also understand it well. To my surprise, the teacher started to tell them the story of Jesus. While she told them the birth of Jesus and how the angel appeared to Mary, the children were greatly moved, and also, the belief that the Holy Spirit came upon Mary from God was an awesome thing for them to listen to. The appearance of an angel to tell Joseph about the birth of Jesus was again a breathtaking incident. It was heavenly for them to listen to every step of the birth of Jesus, and then again, she went on to explain the awesomeness of Jesus's wondrous miracles.

Children enjoyed every bit of the story of Jesus. She also explained to them about the cruel crucifixion of Jesus and the burial, but some people, she said, believed that Jesus rose again. Isn't this an awesome story for the children to enjoy and believe? She went on to describe further the appearance of the angel to the disciples to say that Jesus had risen. I was extremely thrilled to listen to a Muslim teaching so well about Jesus, though she did not say Jesus rose from the dead but said some people did believe He did.

The same thing happened the next day also—the TV did not work. I requested again for a story to be told. The teacher who told the story the day before asked the other teachers to say the story as she had told it the previous day. One teacher stood up and said, since they had heard the story of Jesus the previous day, she would tell the story of Muhammad (peace be upon him). This time, not a single kid was listening—perhaps they had heard it before at home. The Spirit of the Lord is the revealer of all truth.

We continued to get clothes and toys from the main church. I would bring them to school and keep all the extra ones nicely stacked up. The teachers and the local ladies who came to the school would take them to give to some needy neighbor near the house.

The youth from the main church also got excited about the school. They volunteered to come and do some social work for the school. They came on a Saturday morning, cleaned up the school premises, and after lunch, painted Noah's ark and the animals in the ark, a huge picture, on one side of the wall of the TV room. That was great. In the evening, after their dinner, we accommodated them to have a good night's rest in our house and the house of some church members. They participated in the church worship by singing and choreographing on Sunday morning.

To my surprise, on a fine Monday morning, kids in three buses and four young ladies got into the school, and they said they wanted to join us. Was this a blessing of God in multiplication? Yes, indeed. I happily welcomed them. We had to buy some more kids' chairs, some more colorful tables, and make space for them. I had no issues with the new ladies. They were good to me, respected me, and they loved me and knew I loved them too. They could have easily said, "You are an outsider. Why are you doing this? You leave and we will take care of it." I did understand in my life in Oman as a career person that the best tool of evangelism is the "love of Jesus," which should flow in us and manifest in us. When this love is missing, and if we just want to win them for Christ, it may not work.

An Egyptian teacher always told me, "I have a feeling you are sent by God." The teachers also loved the kids. There was a great, love-bound relationship that existed. It was a great blessing to use these young girls who had finished thirteen years of their education but had nothing to do and were just whiling their times away at home. I never had a casual conversation with them, never got myself involved in jokes or fun. Everything was duty-bound, passion-oriented. It was easy for me to assist the teachers in teaching, as I had the experience of teacher training for thirteen years.

We invited a local friend of mine and her sister to our house for dinner. After school, I went home, cooked a very delicious Indian dish and all the dishes to go with it. After dinner, we sat down for a time of conversation. I told them all about Christ and also about the resurrection. The redemptive plan of Jesus in His crucifixion, death, and burial was told to them. They listened to it, but not a word was said. I was tired and frustrated after they left. With all the trouble I took, if only they had reacted to what I told them, I would have been satisfied to some extent at least; I only had to tell my sweet Jesus, "God, You are too slow."

The nursery school for small children from age three to seven was no more a small one; it was now a big school, with five classes and eight teachers, three buses with three drivers, and one four-wheel drive. Praise God! But still, there was no permission from the government and there was no signboard. Anything could happen to me for this kind of illegal project, but I was bold. All these children must have grown now. I wonder how the teachers are. I wish to visit them, given the opportunity. Will I see them all in heaven? Well, we have prayed for them every day. Amen.

We also had very good sets of uniforms for the children, and also two sets of dresses for the teachers, as per their cultural fittings. The teachers were extremely happy about this. I am sure of the parents also being happy with all this. Especially the children singing English songs. The toys and the nice clothing given by the capital were given to many low-income class of Omani children. Oman is a rich country, but still, there will always be some needy children.

All went well. The news about the school went far and wide too. At about ten sharps in the morning, I was getting the orange juice for the children, poured it into glasses, and arranged them on a tray. I was just carrying the tray to the classroom when suddenly I noticed about seven Omani men and an Omani lady entering the school. My heart missed a beat. I thought it was not good for me to stay there, so I kept the tray of juice on the table and started walking out of the school. The gentleman who was first in the line, recognizing me as the person in charge of all the mischief that was going on there, requested me not to leave; he told me that I should stay back.

They were the governors and the directors of different departments of education and towns. I was in deep trouble! They went room by room, but I never went with them. I was just sitting on my seat, tight, waiting to hear the outcome of it. Maybe the teachers answered all their questions. They must have asked a lot of questions about the library, which had a lot of National Geography, and all the games that they had; they must have seen all the exhibits, the huge painting of Noah's ark.

They believed in the Old Testament. They would say, "Prophet Abraham," "Prophet Noah," etc. Whatever, I was not called, and I never attempted to see them or talk to them. After staying there for more than two hours spent in conversation, they left one by one. All of them greeted me goodbye. I just nodded and gave a smile. I did not even bother to ask the teachers what they said or what they asked. I thought it was better to be silent on the issue.

The next day, the lady whom I was looking for and longed to have an appointment with called me and told me the name of the school would be Bait Namu Al Tafel, meaning "house of the youth." She surprised me by telling me that the members who visited the school the previous day wanted me to start many more schools like that. Therefore, I must take my passport to the department to get my visa changed over to the ministry. My answer to her was "no"! She pressurized me a little bit, told me it was good for me, but I said I should move on. When asked why, I told her my husband was moving, so I should move on too.

I left all the toys, bicycles, outdoor slides, seesaws, air conditioners, and all the furniture in the school itself, with the desire that I built it for the locals and so I would leave it for them. I did bring only a doll, as a keepsake. I made a picture of myself with all the children around me. I am not sure what happened to it. I had it in my house and never found it. It disappeared. Now, when I look back, I feel sad for these teachers. I am not sure what happened to them, if they are married or continued to work in the same school. I am not sure.

Children, of course, could have joined another school and are now grown-up. How I wish to visit them and see how big they have grown. The owner, of course, was very sad that I was leaving. He told me he was not going to rent that house out to the teachers if I was not going to be there. Maybe he feared he would not get the rent from them. If the ministry took over it, they would perhaps pay better rent.

After a few days, the teachers traveled to Dubai, where I was, and they came to our house. I wondered why they wanted to see me. They asked me what to do with all the things I had left behind. If I left it for them, who would be in charge of all that? I took this opportunity to tell them all those things belonged to the one who narrated the story of Jesus. She narrated the whole biblical story, and while she did that, she also meant it and believed it. I appreciated the teacher's faithfulness in letting me decide, and they were happy with my decision.

In appreciation of my work, the Toyota top local guy gave me a brand-new car on a discount rate and a letter of commendation. This year, I met an Omani student in ASU who came from the same town, Sohar. I told him that I was the founder of the school Bait Namu Al Tafel, and he was all excited to hear about that. I told him I did have all the pictures on it to show to him. He was all excited about it. It was good to hear from him that it still exists.

I went to the house of one of these teachers and observed their culture of hosting a guest. They would have all kinds of perfumes in a tray, and also, they had a frankincense burner. They would burn the frankincense and hold it under the skirt (dress) of the guest. They would also spray some perfumes all over. All the ladies would sit down, mostly in a circular manner, and then they would give us some dates to eat. And a small cup of very strong coffee to drink that was called kava. If one did not want the coffee, the sign to say no was to shake the cup.

If both the husband and wife were invited to their house, the husband would go and join the men in one room, and the wives would get together in another room. If we were invited for food, lots of rice would be brought in a huge tray with lots of meat in it. All those who would be eating would have to take from that huge tray and eat. The host or the hostess would keep turning the rice over and over to get the meat from the bottom of the tray.

The missionaries who went to Oman from the Reformed Church of Oman were closely connected to the top guys and Sultan himself. They went there about one-hundred-plus years back, when they did not even have air conditioner. They would sleep during the heat of 103 degrees Fahrenheit, sprinkling water on the palm leaves on the rooftops. They would have a big courtyard in the center of their rooms where they would keep sprinkling water for cooling. Dr. Wells Thoms was a great missionary doctor who had been to all the towns on the east coast with his mobile medical hospital, treating the sick people and sharing the gospel. We met an elderly Omani who told us that he knew Dr. Wells Thoms very well. He said Dr. Wells Thoms would treat the sickness of the people even if they did not give him money. Most of the missionaries reached out to the rich and the poor, but in parallel to them, with no choice of meeting, the rich could only reach the middle and the lower middle class.

My Brother and the Bishop

My brother two years older than me met a serious accident on the road and fell asleep in the Lord on the spot. His wife was suffering from fourth-stage brain cancer. Doctors gave her time until August 2019. He was always next to her bed, nursing her and pouring out his love on her. He sold his car, for he would no more drive with her. He loved me the most, even while he was very young; he sold old newspapers and bought a pair of knitting needles for me.

He visited me in Oman on the way to India from Bahrain. I would never share my matters with him, but he would know all about me by observation and react to it favorably. He visited all our fellowships, and just before he went, he made three observations: (1) "I have not seen a pastor like Ernest, who gives so much of individual attention to the congregation." (2) "He drives a lot. Do something about it." (3) "He seems to enjoy his job. Don't disturb him."

By this time, there were some changes among the Reformed Church Pastors for the interior, so Ernest continued to cover up that place for a short while. We had a meeting with the Bishop again. Whenever he came from Cypress, where his headquarters was, he would make it a point to meet us over a cup of coffee. I did tell him my brother's observation, and also, I told him, "Bishop, given an opportunity, I will take him out of Oman. He is driving a lot." Once again, as before, the bishop did not say a word.

After a few months, the Bishop saw us again and asked Ernest to apply for the chaplaincy post in Sharjah, United Arab Emirates. Well, Ernest did apply, and after a certain number of times of his interview, he got the job. Here again, in the interview, they asked me if I would take up the responsibility of the Sunday school. I said yes, but I should have perhaps asked for a small salary. Ernest was accepted as the priest of St. Martin's Church, with a good salary, the car free, the gas free, the house free, furniture provided, phone provided, water and electricity free, and good health insurance paid. Then what more? All free! We had only to spend on eating. Well, I said, "If that is what is given, anybody would like to be a priest."

Ernest was not happy to move. He kept on asking me, "Should we go there because the salary is good? Is it God's will that we move?" While I was most willing to move because I did not want Ernest to drive so hard, I tried to convince him in so many ways, but he would not get convinced. Finally, the bishop told the senior chaplain in the main church that Ernest was selected to be the priest in Sharjah and would be moving shortly. I suppose it was the duty of the bishop to inform them as well. Then the chaplain began to encourage Ernest to move on and they would take care of the sheep that he had nourished—those were their same wordings. Thereby, Ernest had no option but to leave. We had to hand over to the senior chaplain all the responsibilities.

The fortunate things that happened were, during the same year, many of the hospital staff were recruited in Ireland, UK, and US hospitals. So that particular summer, most of them left, and it lessened the sadness of saying goodbye to all of them, mainly because they were also moving. It was not easy to wind up all the small house fellowships and the two houses at the end of our mission work. We had to give away many things.

We carried all my Sunday school materials and the huge load of books that Ernest had and distributed all our furniture for four different places. And we moved on.

In conclusion, the most important things that we learned from our missionaries in the past in Arab-friendly attitude are thus (Van Perusem Mission World, 1920–1921):

1. The village must not only be visited but also worked.
2. Introduce innovations to suit the oriental.
3. Prayers are unintelligible to the average Arab.
4. Three short prayers are better than one long prayer.
5. Repetitions are a secret to success.
6. Upstairs are not to be used for religious purposes.
7. Worship is not acceptable sitting on chairs.
8. Lady worshippers are to be dressed modest, better if their heads are covered.
9. The worship hall should always be on the ground floor.
10. It is a necessary to have Sunday school for children, inspiring them to love the Lord by narrating biblical stories through pictures. For today's children are tomorrow's citizens and leaders.
11. It is better to make a friend than make a sale of Scripture. The former will produce the latter, but not vice versa. Five sales well placed are worth hundreds scattered everywhere.
12. House visiting should not be neglected (Zwemer).
13. Make friends with the headman.
14. Not reading the Bible but the story of the prodigal son.

15. The goodness of Jesus is to be taught by illustrations.
16. The place of meeting should be where Arabs regularly congregated.

In most of our house fellowships, we did remove the chairs and sat on the rugs to worship the Lord.

Fuller Seminary

While I was working with the Ministry of Education, I would get a two-month summer break from the schoolwork every academic year. It was a golden opportunity for us to visit India every summer. That was a great break to be back at home and visit our parents. The Ministry of Education gave us two months' salary before we left for our summer break. We would always have fun, saying, "A bagful of money." They would give us all in all three months' salary, inclusive of the salary on April, May, and June. Positively, we needed a bag to fill the currency in, until they started sending the currency to our bank accounts. It took some time for them to do so. In those days, it was not a practice. This technology did not exist then. In the sixth year of our summer vacation, we thought we would visit the United States.

The dream of Ernest had always been to study theology in Fuller Seminary. It was a well-known seminary for all the Intercollegiate Evangelical Union of Students. Some of our friends were studying there. Fuller Theological Seminary is a multidenominational evangelical Christian seminary in Pasadena, California, with regional campuses in the western United States. The seminary has 2,897 students from ninety countries and 110 denominations (Wikipedia). We did not want to waste our trip by going there. Therefore, we got connected to Fuller Seminary and found out that there were summer intensive courses in Islam by the professor Dr. Dudley Woodbury.

We registered to audit the programs. The immigration was happy to know that Ernest, being an engineer, preferred to go study in a seminary. Therefore, it was easy to obtain a visa for both of us. Both of us registered to audit the courses on Islam on our first day in the US. We were happy to attend the classes. We were not sure why the professor took interest in Ernest. After the class, the professor spoke to Ernest, saying he could credit the course and he would sponsor that. As a result of that, Ernest, misunderstanding what the professor said, studied two other subjects.

When we got back to Oman, we had huge credit to pay for two other subjects, and one particular subject was paid by the professor and we had to pay for two. The next Sunday, as we were getting back home from the church, one British brother came running to us and told us that he had some extra money with him and the Lord seemed to tell him to give that to us. We were amazed at God's intervention and the encouragement for Ernest to continue his studies.

There was another sister in the Lord, by the name of Sister Vivian Stacy; she was a great writer and a missionary for Pakistan. She got in touch with us through Interserve. She wanted to visit us in Oman. During her visit, we arranged for her to visit all our house churches and give the gospel from an Islamic perspective, for her specialization was on Islam. We thought she was a missionary in Pakistan and she should be looked after by us very well. So we got her new Pakistani dresses stitched, and whenever she came with the flask to our kitchen, I would know she needed tea, so I would fill her flask with tea. She was a great inspirer for Ernest to finish his graduation in Islam in Fuller Seminary.

Thereafter, we went to Fuller Summary during all our summer vacations. Ernest would do all the intensives in Fuller in Islamic studies. While Ernest attended the classes, I would also attend the classes sometimes. Most of the time, I would do all his library work. I would sit in the library and read all the historic Islamic books and make some notes for Ernest; mostly, I would copy all his needed text materials for him to compile and do his assignments. Amazingly, I would find the books for his reference. I was never in the habit of looking at a catalog or looking into computers for books. God would take me to the right floor and the right shelf where the books were. It was an amazing God's guidance, as the Fuller library was a huge one, with five floors and an added basement to it.

Fuller Seminary had a great library. I went through many of the Islamic books and was highly motivated to work among the Muslim teachers and students in Oman. On Sundays, we would walk down to Lake Avenue Church in Pasadena. We rented apartments in Providence Mission Home during our two months' stay there. It was a great place to live with other missionaries of the world and fellowship with them. The basement was an excitement there. Trader Joe's would send in groceries and all kinds of fruits and vegetables and leave them at the basements, and we were asked to pick up whatever we needed. This was a blessing, which reduced and saved a little bit of our grocery-shopping time.

Those days were precious days, to walk down to the library and in the halls of Fuller Seminary with all pride of being great scholars yet not being one. The most enjoyable experience was to make appointments with the professors and to have chats with them. Every professor was most humble and respected the students with high regard.

The subject I liked most, other than Islamic studies, was spiritual mapping, the knowledge of which I consider to be the most important, to pray against the dark forces on a particular country. The next subject, of course, is the study of demography, the composition of a particular changing structure of human populations. That would help in adopting a parallel acculturalization in evangelism. It was interesting to go through many such books, as I had plenty of time at my hand, while Ernest was busy in his studies. I also read the Qur'an from page to page; that gave me a better understanding of Christianity and Islam in comparison. I strongly believe that every Muslim should read the Bible and every Christian should read the Qur'an to understand each other's beliefs better. This is my observation and suggestion.

A day before leaving Fuller Seminary, Ernest would submit all his assignments and we would walk out of the seminary saying, *"Operation successful!"*

"The LORD is nigh unto all them that call upon him, to all that call upon him in truth. He will fulfill the desire of them that fear him: he also will hear their cry and will save them" (Ps. 145:18–19 KJV).

We Move to Sharjah (United Arab Emirates)

His Highness Sultan bin Muhammad Al-Qasimi, commonly known as Sheikh Sultan III, is the sovereign ruler of the Emirate of Sharjah and is a member of the Federal Supreme Council of the United Arab Emirates.

Sharjah is the third largest emirate in the United Arab Emirates and is the only one to have landed on both the Persian Gulf and the Gulf of Oman. The emirate covers 2,590 square kilometers (1,000 square miles), which is equivalent to 3.3 percent of UAE's total area, excluding the islands. It has a population of over 1,400,000 (2015). The city lies some 170 kilometers (110 miles) away from the UAE capital city of Abu Dhabi.

The Emirate of Sharjah comprises the city of Sharjah (the seat of the emirate) and other minor towns and enclaves. The city of Sharjah, which overlooks the Persian Gulf, has a population of 519,000 (2003 census estimate). Sharjah City borders Dubai to the south and Ajman to the north. Conservative Sharjah is the only emirate in UAE in which the sale of alcohol is prohibited, although its consumption in one's own home is permissible if one has a valid alcohol license (as is the transportation of alcohol between the place of sale and the home). The only place where this prohibition is relaxed is in the members-only sporting club the Sharjah Wanderers.

Sharjah also maintains the strictest decency laws in UAE, introduced in 2001, with a conservative dress code required for both men and women. Mixing between unmarried men and women is illegal: "A man and a woman who are not in a legally acceptable relationship should not be alone in public places, or in suspicious times or circumstances," according to a booklet published by the municipality in 2001. The Emirate of Sharjah offers an inviting combination of culture, heritage, art, and outdoor activities. To admire the rare artifacts at the Museum of Islamic Civilization and visit the art area for a taste of traditional and contemporary art.

A walk through the heart of Sharjah will reward visitors with a glimpse into history, while outdoor enthusiasts can enjoy an exciting four-wheel drive through the dunes before relaxing on the white beaches or snorkeling through the clear blue waters offshore. The fort was originally constructed in 1820 by the then ruler of Sharjah, Sheikh Sultan bin Saqr Al Qasimi. It was partially demolished in January 1970, and the restoration of Sharjah Fort commenced in January 1996 and was completed in April 1997 (Wikipedia).

Sharjah Christians account for 13 percent of the total population of the United Arab Emirates. The country has

Oriental Orthodox and Eastern Orthodox churches along with Protestant and Roman Catholic churches.

St. Philip the Apostle Russian Orthodox Church is a Russian Orthodox church located in Sharjah. The church is the biggest in the country, with an area of 1,800 square meters and a capacity of twenty thousand worshippers. The church opened on Saturday, August 13, 2011 (Wikipedia).

St. Martin's Church in Sharjah, United Arab Emirates

St. Martin's Anglican Church follows the Anglican diocese of Cyprus and the Gulf, under the leadership of Bishop Michael Lewis. In the UAE, the church partakes in the chaplaincy of Dubai, Sharjah, and the northern emirates. St. Martin's Anglican Church is part of the diocese of Cyprus and the Gulf, under Bishop Michael Lewis.

St. Martin's Anglican Church runs various ministries, where each ministry concentrates on a particular group of people—women and men, teens, young adults, and children—as a matter of importance. Experts in all these fields were periodically invited to train the leaders as per their specifications on modern trends and techniques.

The members of the church had taken us to see houses and select one. The lady administrator who helped us to select was a Sri Lankan, who is no more now. One particular house I called a brown house drew my attention. That was a perfect house, where I felt safe, not only from the external fear, but also from all the worries and troubles of the outside world. It was classy and exclusive. We can confidently claim that we felt relaxed. We loved every small detail in it, from its size, design, and location, and we wouldn't have asked for any other house than this. The house had a dark brownish roof and brown walls, as well as brown wooden windows that could be wide-opened on sunny days. I especially love the window in the living room, as it faced the street, where a large palm tree grew, with a beautiful green lawn around it. The windowsill of the window was great enough to display the iconic rocks that I had collected.

The house had four bedrooms, three on the first floor and one on the ground floor. It had one living room, one kitchen, and three bathrooms. However, all rooms were filled with natural light. I loved windows facing the sunny side. There was a huge front grilled patio door with a glass frame that led from the kitchen to the front yard. There was a slightly elevated platform attached to the grilled patio door that was used to "display" the dinner dishes. When we had the opportunity to have dinner outside, during the church parties, the master bedroom was upstairs, and we had a huge grilled window as we headed downstairs. That gave us a great view of the outside world.

We got all our luggage and started settling in. Since there were three bedrooms upstairs, we put all our unpacked suitcases in the third bedroom. A big welcome party was also arranged between all the three Anglican churches, and it was a great party of celebration, with cake-cutting and sumptuous, delicious dinner. The work began. Sunday mornings was when the service was held, and in the evenings, Ernest had to go to Dubai for marriage counseling. We both went to Dubai. While Ernest took the marriage counseling, I used to attend the denominational services held in the church premises and enjoyed the different kinds of services.

One Sunday evening, after the counseling service was over, we came home at 9:00 p.m. Our bedroom was upstairs. I took my handbag with me upstairs, as we had to call our friends in Oman. We had still kept in touch with our friends in Oman. My phone was in the bag. After the phone call, Ernest wanted to sleep by 9:30 p.m. and asked me to put off the light. He said he wanted to get up early in the morning. For him, getting up early was at 3:30 or 4:00 a.m. So, we went to sleep. I was also up by 3:30 a.m. and was thanking God that I had some money in my bag and I could use them for my offering. Meanwhile, I heard Ernest calling out for me from downstairs, and I ran down. He said that we were robbed. *The thieves had come in by breaking open the front door!*

The guest bathroom was on the right side of the front entrance. We went in there; my Bible, my handbag, my phone, and all my credit cards, identity card, and health ID card were all kept in the sink of the bathroom. Water was filled, and the stopper was put in so that the sink retained the water. The Bible was fully immersed in the water. *All the pages were swollen up, and the scripts were erased.*

We called the Sharjah church administrator, the Dubai church administrators, and the caretaker of the church. All of them came in. They called the police, and the police came in too. They went around to check if things were intact. We found a piece of thick thread rolled on a pair of scissors picked up from our drawer in the kitchen. Perhaps they got it to strangle us in case we woke up. We didn't think they went up on the first floor.

In any case, they asked us to go check the upstairs. As we went into the third bedroom, where we had kept all our luggage, we found four suitcases were missing. We were happy that none of the laptops were taken, for they contained all our details. The church administrator believed that the burglars might have thrown the suitcases in the corners of the roads if they did not contain any valuable material. All my credentials were in one of the boxes, and in another box were Ernest's surplus pure silver chain and a beautiful cross. Two other suitcases had nothing valuable in them. I was least bit worried about my credentials, for it was all God's will, I thought. The administrator who went to look for it came back without finding anything.

Then, we went to our bedroom and found out that our video camera was not there. It was clear then that the burglars had come to the first floor and onto our bedroom. Another indication that they had come to our bedroom was that my handbag, which I had taken up with my phone, was immersed in the water in the sink in the guest bathroom on the ground floor. The phone I had used to call our friends in Oman was taken up to call them, and the burglars had brought it down along with the purse. Ernest had his phone with him, and as the church paid for it, he would use it for church purposes only. It was safe.

I wondered how there was no noise of them coming into the house. Normally, Ernest is an early bird, so he sleeps early. Whereas I sleep very late at night and get up late. I am a light sleeper; any sound will disturb me and wake me up. I am also in the habit of going to the bathroom during the night. That night, I had had a deep sleep. I wonder how.

The next day, Ernest couldn't give up. He went around the house, and when he went into the compound of the next abandoned house, he found all the four suitcases, and I saw him bringing all the four suitcases, running with the joy of a little kid. Well, all my credentials were there. Praise God they did not need it! Ernest lost his surplus silver chain and the silver cross.

It was all a mystery for me. I just could not imagine how Ernest asked me to turn off the light and wanted to sleep early to get up early. How I went off to sleep early, which I would never do. Nothing disturbed my sleep that day, and I had a deep sleep. All nights before we slept, we locked our bedroom too, and that night, we had never locked. My jewelry and another bag of offering money were also in the cupboard, which they never opened. If they had just opened my cupboard a little bit, they would have found the gold and the money—it was just right in front.

Perhaps the sound of opening the cupboard would have woken us up, and they did not want us to wake up. In any case, it remains a mystery to me how it was that I did not wake up while they were in our bedroom. What if I opened my eyes when they were there? Fear, scream, and whatnot. What would they have done if I had screamed while they were there? Many such thoughts would roll in my mind.

Our two friends from the church came to our house every day to sleep in our house, for the church to realize it was not safe for us to live there. They put a new lock to the door, and they also put a grill for the front door and a grill between the first and the second floor. Only after that, they found the house was safe to live. They let us stay all by ourselves.

I also had a small bag of Omani coins in the bedroom. The burglars had taken it, and after a week of the burglary, the burglars had thrown the bag of coin into our compound. We did not understand why the burglars took away the surplus of the priest. I wonder what they did with it. Of course, they would have made some money out of the silver cross and the silver chain. After a few days, we found my cell phone in the compound of the next abandoned house on the left. It was no use for the burglars as they could not open it without the code.

The church also considered if they should withdraw the house contract from the owner of the house, but since the house belonged to a very top guy of the emirate, they did not want to do that. The street's name was in the name of the top personality. I was curious to see who these burglars were to boldly enter into our bedroom. I did pray to ask God to show them to me. Funny prayer, of course. After several months, there was a knock on the door, and a local CID was there. He said they found the thief and we could see him if we wished to. *I ran to see him. He gave me an awkward smile, and I ran back just as I ran to see him.*

The next Sunday, while Ernest was driving to the church in Dubai for the marriage counselor, a car came and hit his car from the back. Fortunately, one of our church members lived at the same spot on the roadside, and she called others and they all came to help Ernest. I had not gone with Ernest that day.

There was another car accident again for Ernest. As he got out of the Dubai church gate, a car from the left side came in high speed and hit his car hard. Ernest was safe, and the car was written off. This time, a friend of mine had only to say, "Satan is not very happy that Reverend Ernest is here." Driving in Oman was excellent, with the drivers strictly following the traffic rules, but in Dubai, it was not so, because people from other countries followed the traffic rules of their country and the traffic rules of Dubai and would mix rules up. So that was the beginning of our life in Sharjah, Dubai.

The house on the right and our house were twin houses. On a bright evening, a British couple came to our house in search of one big building in which they ran a school. We heard from them that there was one big building before where we lived. And they were running a school there. I was very much curious to ask them if they were the missionaries. I tried to ask them with many questions but could only know that they were brought from the UK to teach and run the school. Those days were the days when they did not have schools for elite children. Now that they did not want that to be a school anymore, they converted it into two villas. But the next house on the left was abandoned.

Our church members who had seen our school in Oman asked me if I was interested in starting a school in Dubai. I was not for it, because the rent there was very expensive, and I knew I would be moving from there. Having started in India, we moved to Oman. Then having started the school in Oman, we moved to Sharjah. Now again, I did not want to start one in Sharjah and move on to another place.

Well, there was another family of five with three children and a couple in the church who had left their hometown and were in Sharjah. They lived near our house. Both husband and wife had no jobs and were finding it difficult to run the family with three children on hand. She was a mathematics teacher, and the husband was a lawyer. She tried to take up a teacher's position in schools, but she was not successful. She approached me to go with her and help her start school. I suggested that she can look into the possibility of finding out the owner of the next abandoned house and perhaps start one there. She took me along with her to find out who the owner was, and after several attempts of visiting several offices, finally we came to one top guy who said the owner could not be revealed.

The church service was excellent. After church service on Sundays, in the evenings, we had great refreshments, managed and organized by two lovely sisters. Ernest just followed the church service as per tradition. There were some issues among the church members, as it would be in all the churches, but we were never told about it. The two church people who were sleeping in our house every day after the robbery did not tell us also, but the bishop knew about it, and even he did not mention it.

The bishop must have thought that Ernest could sought out the issue, which could be one of the reasons the bishop wanted him there. Well, we had a little bit of a struggle, but it was negligible. The best thing that Ernest did was to keep them all busy with a lot of workload on them. He started all kinds of activities wherein all got busy and there was no scope for church politics. One of the senior members of the church, referring to us, said, "These two are not afraid of anybody. They are bold enough to take bold steps, and they move on."

The church building was given by the ruler to the Anglican Church. It is the responsibility of the Anglican Church to maintain the church, and they can also rent out the building to other congregations. It was Ernest's responsibility to coordinate between all the congregations and meet with them, if they needed help, and provide for them their necessaries, sometimes even to sort out their disputes. About eighty-four congregations were meeting in the church complex.

Fridays were great days, sightseeing to have the pleasure of seeing a huge multitude of worshippers walking in and out of the church gate. When I heard the great worship of all the people in the congregations, sometimes praying loudly and pleading for God to answer their prayers, I was reminded of the verse Ezekiel 22:30 (KJV), "And I sought for a man among them, that should make up the hedge, and stand in the gap before me for the land, that I should not destroy it: but I found none." *My question to my Lord was, "Is there no one here to stand in the gap?"*

The great success of this ministry was the Holy Spirit. Our fellowship with the Lord Jesus, which would be vertical, would also lead us to have a successful horizontal fellowship. I would only see Ernest taking all the issues of the church to the Lord. He always spent a lot of time praying before he preached. The congregation did appreciate his sermon and could see the Lord bringing in changes in their lives. The family relationship improved. Those who were addicted gave up addiction. We did have great singers for worship. We could sense the power of the Lord when they worshipped. Praise the Lord!

Friday Services

About fifty or sixty attended the Sunday service; therefore, the council of the church wanted to start a Friday service. Fridays and Saturdays were general holidays declared by the government, and their holy day was Friday, being an Islamic country. Therefore, a church service started in a small room that could seat about forty people. About twenty-five to thirty people were attending. The service was an extremely Spirit-filled family type of contained fellowship, but the church grew slowly and the room got filled up, so we had to take up the main hall.

Sunday service was mostly a traditional one, and the Friday service was contemporary service. Friday service slowly began to grow. Some attended both the Friday service and the Sunday service. Ernest was much blessed in his sermons. I have also heard a lot of appreciation for his message, as it was most relevant to their personal lives. I heard of them saying, "Man looks so insignificant, but on the pulpit, he speaks as God speaks." We praise God for this.

Apart from the church administration, Ernest was also responsible for conducting marriages. The marriage counseling, which was held in Dubai on Sundays, also moved to the Sharjah church. Ernest was extremely happy about this. Many from Ethiopia and other countries like Germany, Italy, Africa, and the Philippines, though not many from India, wanted to be married. They were either on a world trip or working in the Emirates and met their partners there and decided to get married.

The greatest opportunity that Ernest enjoyed was to talk to them about his favorite subject, being "born again." He would get acquainted with them by talking to them about their previous life and if they had married previously, and then he would begin to talk to them about the fulfillment in married life in Jesus Christ. He would also lead them to the plan of salvation and the grace of Jesus by explaining to them the redemptive purposes of God. Finally, he would lead them to the sinner's prayer. Luke 15:10 (KJV) says, "Likewise, I say unto you, there is joy in the presence of the angels of God over one sinner that repenteth."

When we moved to the Emirates, there was a massive migrant labor ministry among Indian and Pakistani migrant workers, who make up for more than 50 percent of the labor force. The expatriate workers' population in the UAE is around 90 percent. And the UAE population, 10 percent. The population of the UAE noted for 2016 is 9,157,000 according to UN estimates. Other estimates are as low as 5.7 million but do not take into consideration the high population of immigrants, which are estimated to make up 90 percent of the population.

The passion Ernest had for the work among the migrant workers took a new birth in the Emirates. Coming to know about the existence of several migrant labor camps, Ernest encouraged the members to visit the camps and pray with them. Slowly they did recognize they needed a full-time worker for the camps, and also one who could speak in their language.

So, a selection was made, and slowly it was also recognized that they needed one more.

Therefore, two of them were selected. One was an Indian who could speak and preach in an Indian language, and the other one from Pakistan, who could speak in their language. Both were good speakers, and both were God-fearing. Both of them were ordained as deacons, and finally as priests of the Anglican community. Ernest would also attend these camp meetings. At times, when he could not attend the migrant meetings, he would get the reports from the leaders who attended the meetings.

Some ladies took interest in going to meet the migrant lady workers. That was a great ministry too. The lady leader was a devoted lady, full of passion for the Lord. A great preacher and dedicated to the Lord's work. She would take along with her some other ladies from the church. The deacons who were in charge of the men's work were driving them to the lady's camp. Sometimes the place of the habitation was not hygienic; even then, they would take pleasure in going and give them the gospel. Another gentleman took great interest in men's migrant work. He would team up the young adult men and go along to the migrant camps.

Christmas celebration among all these migrant camps was a great one. They were given Christmas gifts with delicious dinner. The meaning of Christmas was always explained. Some of the church members and we both would attend all these celebrations. All the migrant workers would be given opportunities to exhibit their talents in singing or expressing their opinions about these fellowship meetings.

Since these migrant laborers were away from their families and their children, they were extremely happy to have us visit them, talk to them, comfort them, and above all, lead them toward Christ, with whom they could get connected and develop a father-child relationship, wherein they could pour out all their loneliness and problems to their Father and be strengthened to make a better living. It was an amazing work of the Holy Spirit, wherein most of them came to know the salvation grace of Jesus. Every week, about ten to sixteen would come to the Friday service to witness their love for Jesus. We have not heard about many of them now, but we hear one of them is planting churches in India. We praise God for that.

So, there were two buses, two pastors, one lady worker, with many other church members, along with Ernest, all set to work with hundreds of migrant workers in the United Arab Emirates, to pray with them and to take them to the grace of the Lord Jesus Christ. The results were great!

St. Martin's Villa

Our house was called St. Martin's Villa, mostly because the church paid the rent. We had a youth fellowship on Fridays after the Friday church service. There were about fifteen to eighteen youth, with great youth leadership. The leader, an engineering student, was always coming up with new ideas and was immensely filled with passion for the Lord. And also, was keen on outreach programs. All the youth respected her and cooperated with her in all that she wanted to do. Once, she came up with an idea to invite all the youth in the Emirates, and as a result, there were about fifty of them approximately.

To my surprise, one student came from my father's village. I made a big mistake in not taking her contact address; maybe I would have known more about my father or his relatives who lived in that village.

Ernest was very particular in handling the Bible studies for them on Fridays before the church service. He prayerfully led them to Christ and was assured that all knew the Lord as their personal Savior. This particular set of youth was also talented in choreography, singing, and dramatics. They were excellent. They would compose all the talented activities and practice it themselves and exhibit them in the church programs. The lady adviser for them, with her husband, was always with them, guiding them and assisting them whenever they needed them. I told them that she loved them more than her two children.

Every winter, we had a barbecue on Thursday nights. The families brought marinated meat, and the men barbecued them. The families kept on eating along with the salads. Those who ate a lot proved it by collecting their chicken bones. The one who had the most would get a prize.

The women's fellowship was on Wednesday mornings. We studied the books of the Bible. The leader was an elderly Pakistani lady. She did a great job, and she had studied the Bible well. We prayed for the church regularly. I always considered the prayers of the women of the church as the backbone of the church. I was the first pastor's wife in the church who was not the treasurer of this women's fellowship. Money was what I kept away from. For me, keeping money in the purse sometimes appeared to be keeping Satan in the purse.

Prayer for the church is the backbone of the church, when the members of the church came together at the feet of Jesus, humbling themselves in unity, with the same mind, as in Philippians 2:2 (KJV), "Fulfil ye my joy, that ye be likeminded, having the same love, being of one accord, of one mind." Many prayers were answered, and the church grew in numbers. We met every Thursday for prayer and worship. There were no time restrictions. We would go on as long as we wanted. Friends brought all their prayer requests, and every one of them was answered. We praise God.

The unity of the Spirit was excellent. I have not enjoyed such worship and prayer since we left the Middle East. I would long to have one like it. "Finally, be ye all of one mind, having compassion one of another, love as brethren, be pitiful, be courteous" (1 Pet. 3:8 KJV). After the prayer, we had a sumptuous dinner cooked by the ladies. They were such great friends of ours; they would clean the entire living room and the kitchen, keep all the furniture before they left neat and tidy. They made me feel comfortable and happy.

Visiting Prison

Visiting prison was a heart-churning experience. Men visited men's prison, and the ladies visited the ladies' prison. A society with high core values does not tolerate social evils. The social evils will be punished. We met with the inmates of the prison and had a conversation with them in-depth. We would take all the necessities, like toothpaste, soap, and some undergarments, as per their needs. They were happy that somebody was there to hear them and be sympathetic toward them. All of us do sin and come short of the glory of God, but He is faithful and just to forgive all our sins, and He would consider us as His children. They did recognize their mistakes now that they were in prison. They would tell us what exactly their mistake was and repent. We would together ask God for forgiveness, say the sinner's pray, and receive the grace of God and obtain salvation.

Four Young Sri Lankan Girls

Two or three months after we took over Sharjah chaplaincy's work, about four o'clock in the evening, I was busy unpacking and arranging, trying to beautify the house. I had a call from Ernest, who was in the church office. In that call, he asked me to go to church to pray for some girls who they believed were possessed. I was not ready to go there, as there was no spiritual preparedness for that kind of prayer, but I had no choice in the matter, as the girls were already there.

So, I went. There were also other ladies to pray for the issue. Girls were there. I believe they were tailors in a company. Not sure how their inmates came to know they were possessed and how four could be possessed in a particular place. Were they truly possessed, or were they not happy about the existing condition in the place where they lived? I was not sure.

All four of them looked undernourished. They did not look happy at all. Pathetic, indeed. We started worshipping the Lord. Our favorite worship song was requesting the Holy Spirit of the living God to "fall afresh on me." As we started singing and worshipping the Lord with a prayerful attitude, one by one they started falling. One fell on the bench that was in the room, all her hair out, scattered, turning the face sideways, left to right. The other one started moving all around the room like a snake, with both her palms held together, up over her head, like the cobra snake. Our concentration was on this girl. Two other girls were just on the ground, rolling. I am not sure how they could all fall at the same time—perhaps the gush of the Holy Spirit, which helped us to pray.

The impure spirit shook the man violently and came out of him with a shriek.

> And the spirit cried, and rent him sore, and came out of him: and he was as one dead; insomuch that many said, He is dead. But Jesus took him by the hand and lifted him, and he arose. (Mark 9:26–27 KJV)

> The spirit shrieked, convulsed him violently, and came out of him. (Mark 1:26 KJV)

We prayed for them, prayed till they were all right. We did not go near to pray for them one by one; perhaps we should have done that. I was most unprepared for this task.

After they got up, we sent them to the church below, in the main hall. It was a Sri Lankan Pentecostal church, most suitable for these lovely young Sri Lankan girls. The church had just begun the service, well-timed. We praise God for every blessing! Amen!

As I write this, I remember having visited *Dargah Yousufain. Also, Yousuf Baba Sharif Baba Dargah is a dargah in Hyderabad, India,* where two Muslim Sufi saints, named Hazrath Syed

Shah Yousufuddin and Syed Shah Sharifuddin, are buried. Some Muslims believe these Sufi saints, though died and buried, have healing power. Many such possessed people are brought to this place to lie down there for healing. Exactly at 6:00 p.m., a loud bell went ringing; at that exact time, the evil possession in the people lying there was manifested. Each one who was believed to be possessed would be rolling in different ways. Here again, I am not sure how and why the bell at six o'clock affected all of them all at once. We boldly went around, seeing and praying for all of them, though it was scary. No change was noticed. *May the grace of our Lord Jesus deliver them in His redemptive power of grace.*

Sunday School

My Sunday school work in Oman was simple. I would go from town to town with Ernest. While he took the Bible studies for the adults, I would take the Sunday school for their children. During that time, I would make them sing worship songs with action. Help them to mean what they were singing and then narrate the Bible story, with the help of the book with relevant flashcards bought in Christian bookstores. I always had great fun teaching the little ones. But it was not the same in Sharjah, where we had seventeen children in Sunday service, and more than thirty children in the Friday service. I had to look into a better curriculum for a systematic study of the Bible that met both the young and the old children.

Therefore, I looked into the curriculum to pick up a good one. But I failed to appreciate even one. According to me, each one had some defects. I had certain criteria in mind. I wanted the children to use the Bible, and I wanted them to understand the Bible sequentially, not jumping from story to story on a thematic basis but knowing the Bible as a whole. I did not want the children to learn the Bible on culture-to-culture value. I wanted them to learn the Bible in-depth, in a simpler manner, and learn the Bible verses by heart, as they would help them at the time of need. While they learned, I wanted them to enjoy what they learned.

For this purpose, I selected a psychological approach on insight learning. It was easy for me to pick up this methodology, as I had completed a master's in educational psychology. Furthermore, I was in a research program with many practical teachings to high school children in the learning process, where we believed in the problem-solving method. Kohler found that once the apes discovered they could not reach the fruit, they stopped and thought about how they might solve the problem.

After some time, they were able to use the tools at their disposal to solve the problem and reach the fruit. Kohler called this cognitive process of insight learning. Learning by insight means sudden grasping of the solution, a flash of understanding, without any process of trial and error. This theory is also called the Gestalt theory of learning. The word Gestalt is from the German language and means "whole." According to Tolman, in all learning, some intelligence is at work. It is the learner who actively participates in the act of getting new experience. He organizes his perceptions and observations and gives meaning to them. It is his whole mind that perceives, constructs, and reconstructs experience.

The primary goal of the Gestalt theory is to encourage the brain to view not just the whole but also the parts that make up that whole. For example, when someone is looking at a tree, is he just staring at this tree, or does he also see the leaves, the branches, and the trunk? The whole and the sum of its parts are two entirely different things, and learning can be achieved if learners can cognitively process how parts can make up this whole. Problem-solving presents learning with understanding using Gestalt principles. This learning is remembered for a long time and can be applied to other situations.

These psychological principles were merged to the practicality of a system in producing the Pearl Sunday school curriculum. The title of the curriculum, Pearl, was given to me by God based on the verse Matthew 13:45–46 (KJV), *"Again, the kingdom of heaven is like unto a merchant man, seeking goodly pearls: Who, when he had found one pearl of great price, went and sold all that he had, and bought it." Children are fine pearls of great value, and we, as teachers, need to do everything that we can to find these great pearls of value for the kingdom of God.*

Every word of the divine scriptures is like a pearl of great value. In this Sunday school curriculum, the Pearl, I have tried my best to bring the divine scriptures, the pearl of great value, to the great pearls of value, who are the children. These great values need to merge in establishing the kingdom of God. The Pearl Sunday school curriculum is a three-year curriculum, during which I would introduce the Bible to the children in a systematic way. The teaching is based on "insight learning," where it is believed that children learn by insight. The tool of which is problem-solving puzzles.

The grids, based on teaching highlights, are meant for the teachers' use. Insights are the main points of the Bible story. Each insight has an application. The teachers are at liberty to interpret the applications as the Lord leads. If the applications are in third person, they should be applied to the first person, "I" or "we." The students will be able to apply at least one of the applications to his or her life situation. Every "insight" should be explained with the applications during the lesson itself. Children tend to lose their concentration if the application is pushed off after the narration of the story. It would be great if the day's Bible story is well narrated in the devotion time, meant for all the combined classes. The students need to directly use the Bible to learn the day's lesson.

The activities conclude the lesson, and it would reinforce the learning. The teacher may have to explain the activities or help them to start. If an activity is not completed, it can be given as homework. The answers to every activity should be checked and discussed.

Scripture references meant for meditation should be read by the teacher in his/her preparation time. Students should positively bring a Bible to Sunday school to read the day's lesson.

Teachers have to be sensitive to the learning ability of the students and modify the lesson accordingly. If they don't have time or are not interested, the pictures should be observed and discussed by all the children and the teacher.

The most crucial aspect of every lesson is how much of it is applied to the life situation of the child that would result in a change in attitude and behavior that is acceptable, a Christlikeness.

To begin with, I had three beautiful young sisters with me. They were born and brought in Dubai. They could not go to schools because of financial issues. Their grandfather was a devoted man and was a very successful businessman initially, and as the days went by, he lost his business. They were Anglicans, and therefore they attended our church. They lived very close to our house, and it was very convenient for them to come home. We worked together in coordination and great love for one another. They were excellent at typing and creative work. Above all, they loved the Lord.

On the ground floor, the guest room became a workshop for me. I had all that I wanted there.

The lady from Los Angeles called me her sister. I loved my sisters, as I had no sisters of my own. Another friend of mine who was in charge of wayfarers sent all the Sunday school materials and the teaching aides through this sister of mine to Dubai by post. It was great to pick up all the ideas and compare with all the materials that they were sending. Thus, I gained some experience. There was also another gentleman who was an engineer, building railway rails and routes on the computer, who was most willing to help me whenever I wanted.

There was another computer technician who came to our house on a payment basis. He would always shout at me for nothing. I wondered why I should get his shouting, even after paying him. But the last day, when he came, he made peace with me by saying I served food to Ernest whenever and whatever time he came home. That was funny. I think, since it was the last day of his work with us, he was trying to make up for his showers of angry words to me.

An Australian scientist was attending our church. He was a professor in one of the universities in Dubai. He was on the very heavier side. He was telling us that he was mainly a scientist for inventing robots, not a professor of teaching. He was not married, but whenever anybody asked him why he was not married, he would say, "Bring a woman according to Proverbs 31:30 (KJV) which says, "Favor is deceitful, and beauty is vain: but a woman that feareth the LORD, she shall be praised."

We were acquainted with him for only one year, after which he had to leave Dubai and move on. He just dumped all his goods in our house, as it was the house of a pastor. This helped me to furnish my workshop well. I had my big office table, on which a computer, a printer, and a scanner were set. So, I was all set for my task of writing Sunday school books on Gestalt learning of the Bible. I had a lot of cupboards to stack up all my books, videos, CDs, and tapes.

I also went for a graphic design class in Dubai. My teacher would never understand why, during that part of my life, I needed to learn that. Several times he asked that, in indirect ways, my answer would only be that I would be writing Bible lessons for children. I could also buy a set of clip art CDs and a crossword puzzle maker.

My first book was ready to be printed by my friend/sister in Oman who was an encourager in my school project there, and a prayer partner got some unexpected money from her working place. She sent some portion of the money to me, which I lavishly used for printing of the books. I was told that printing of the color books was very expensive; it would be better if I made it black-and-white. My argument was, if the school textbook was in color, why should biblical Sunday school books be black-and-white?

I gave my first book to the printer to print it. I gave him the stick in which I had copied. When he took it and opened it, there was nothing in it. He came home to tell me about it. I opened my computer and found there was nothing in it too. My nephew was there, and he suggested to open the recycle bin, and there it was! The printer had to tell my nephew not to teach me anything; if he did, I might bring the sky down. By this, the printer was only pulling my leg—definitely no feather in my cap. He was also of the opinion why, at that age, I wanted to do all that, why I couldn't take rest and relax. He had to say this to me several times. How would anybody who did not understand the passion of the Lord understand what was going on within me? The Lord helped me to write six major Sunday school books and four minor Sunday school books. They were called Pearl Sunday school curriculum.

The Sunday school on Sundays only had sixteen to twenty children. The Sunday school on Fridays had nearly thirty-five to forty children. They used Pearl books for teaching. The books contained some color pages for younger children and puzzles for older children. It would also be a teacher's guide.

What follow are teachers' comments on the Pearl books.

Whelma M.
Sharjah St. Martin's Church
I taught the Pearl book 4 and book 5.

Good points: Excellent, with memory verse for each lesson. It is teacher-friendly, trustworthy, biblical, enjoyable, and interactive. For teachers, it is again excellent, with Bible portions and then insight, application points, prayer, etc.

I would prefer that children have books like Pearl books, which kids and teachers both can use. From the Pearl books, even a parent can help at home if the child missed out any class.

Points to consider: When I taught them book 5, Peter, they found it easier. Book 4 would be enjoyed more by eleven-plus-year-old kids, as they can understand sin and salvation better. Book 1, small kids might enjoy more than the big kids aged eleven and above. So, all I am trying to say is, books are excellent but would be nice if they are age-appropriate.

I miss your books!

Roseline Charles
Sharjah St. Martin's Church
The Pearl series for Sunday school children, from toddlers to preteens.

I, Roseline Charles, had the privilege to teach children with these books for more than five years for different age groups. It's a book that is so dedicatedly prepared for the children according to their age groups, with a guide for the teachers as well. The children loved it—all the pictures, coloring, and activities, the children enjoyed so much. Step-by-step instructions were very helpful to teach the Word of God to the children in a systematic way. And the importance given to make the children learn the memory verses and stories is a real pearl of great value, which I am sure the children will remember lifelong. I would recommend that every child be allowed to learn the Word of God through these books so that they will remember them forever due to the interesting activities and images representing each story or character in the Bible.

Sophia Kavita Ezra George

I find the Pearl book to be an academic book for the children. By that I mean that every lesson has a teaching point and a learning point. It is interactive, with stories, illustrations, puzzles, etc. The lessons are easy to follow for a chosen age range. The illustrations are high-quality and professional. It's relatable to a wide range of children. After doing the lessons in Pearl, children begin to read, understand, and discuss the Bible more confidently.

Summer Bible School

Apart from Sunday school, the children had great times in vacation Bible school. I did not call it a vacation Bible school; instead, I called it a summer Bible school. I wanted all the children to spend their five days of summer holidays in the church. We would begin in the mornings at seven o'clock, and we will close it at 3:00 p.m. We would have facilities for small kids to lie down and rest while the older ones would be engaged in activities. Some church members volunteered to give breakfast, and others gave lunch, and some others gave midday snacks. In addition to this, we also had cookies and some cold soft drinks in case the smaller children wanted any.

Three days earlier to the SBS, I would take my three young Pakistani sisters shopping. They were great in craftwork. They would buy all the materials required for the craftwork related to the Bible story. I liked the way they discussed every item before they bought it.

There were nearly sixty children, and we divided them area-wise, and accordingly, we sent the buses to bring them. Some parents also cooperated to bring them. The church by now owned two buses, and the two deacons were responsible to bring the children to the church. We also got some nice T-shirts printed. It was great excitement for the children as well as the parents and the teachers. We used the youth to lead them in the singing. Some youth played music too. A set of kids' songs with actions was already selected and printed. Every child would have it with them along with the workbooks. On average, the children would learn about ten Bible-based action songs and some memory verses in connection with a series of five lessons of a biblical hero—for five days.

SBS would have a theme verse and a theme song. We began the days with the theme songs and the theme verse. Then the youth would teach them the songs. I would do the narration of that particular day's Bible story. I would be dramatizing it so that the young and the old kids would understand it well. They would go to their classrooms and follow the timetable scheduled for the day.

They studied on the day's Bible portion with puzzle and discussed them with the teacher. The little ones would color the pictures and recite the memory verse and would have a conversation with the teachers. All the kids, the young and old, would do their craftwork, which would be relevant for the day's Bible portion. The kids below six years would play some games and learn some action songs. If they knew some songs taught by their mothers, they would teach the other children. They would have some fun that way. All these little kids memorized the Lord's Prayer.

After lunch, the younger kids would be put to sleep on the mats provided. The older ones now would get into different groups as per their talents. Some went to dramatics, singing, choreography, etc. I am not sure if I was the first one to introduce the choreography for the worship songs those days. To put all the worship songs sung into action and music so that the worship would come from the bottom of their hearts, bowing down to the holy one in His awesomeness and beauty.

They would then get back to the main hall. I would be in charge of this general session, and they would again sing songs with the help of the youth. Then they would watch a portion of the video of the Bible story they learned that particular day. I would ask them to narrate the Bible verses they learned, class by class, and they would be applauded for that. It was also great to listen to the little kids narrating their memory verse.

My greatest pleasure for that day would be singing and leading them to sing, "God is so good, God is so good, God is so good, is so good to me. He answers prayers, He answers prayers, He answers prayers, is so good to me." I would enjoy singing this from the bottom of my heart. *The thrill, the excitement of leading and singing this song with the children, can never be explained.*

There was a small storeroom on the first floor that was cleared and was made into a prayer room. During the SBS time, an elderly lady and two others would sit there and keep praying. Whenever I was free from SBS sessions, and when I observed things were going smoothly and children were busy with their activities, I would also join them to pray. The intimate fellowship we enjoyed there, and the prayers we said there for the children and the parents, was always enjoyable and would never be forgotten. Oh, how I wish I would sit there to pray again! With the same friends, of course. Whatever we do for the Lord within a short time, we should do it well, with all our heart, mind, spirit, and soul. Once this period was over, we would never get it back, however much we wished.

The next Saturday after the SBS, there would be an event on the competition for all the children who attended the SBS, from the age of three onto the age of sixteen. They would be given a podium with a mic, with an intention that they should be trained for mass communication even at an early age. Moreover, the children enjoyed and took all the pride to speak on a microphone. There would be various completions on the recitation of Bible verses, singing, debating on a scriptural concept, narration on the Bible story they learned in SBS, etc.

Three judges would be seated at the back of the hall to grade each child, and at the end of the program, the children would be rewarded suitably. The chief judge for the competition would pass her/his remarks of encouragement to the children to conclude the event. I would plan and program this event with the help of the teachers. The mothers would also take part in this program in training the children.

The next day of the SBS, all the parents would be invited to visit the church and see all the crafts the children did. One item of each would be displayed outside; all the rest would be kept in packets along with the name tags of the children and displayed. Each parent could pick up their kid's packets.

I would encourage the teachers to give them practice for the Christmas program too so that they would be ready to enact the same at Christmas time. The Christmas program by the children would be another great event in the church. The parents were delighted about the programs held in the church, and as a result, the church grew in numbers. We praise God for this.

Harvest Festival

Men's fellowship was in charge of the harvest festival. When the men's fellowship was started in the church, I was a little apprehensive. I wondered if they would give in to church politics. But to my dismay, they were very much spiritually oriented. They had regular Bible studies on Saturday mornings. The harvest festival was for only one day in October. All the church members would bring the things that they wanted to give to the church. All that they grew also would be brought in. They would hold them in both hands and come into the church in a procession, from outside, while the first hymn was sung, and place it at the altar.

Some would even give money. There would be stalls all around the hall, with games, eats, and sales of all kinds of goodies, which would be organized by the ladies' fellowship. It would be great fun to watch the young and the old enjoying all kinds of eats and games. A lot of money would be collected that day, but that money need not have to go to the main church but could be used for mission work. Therefore, all that money would be sent to many missionaries to underdeveloped countries and to countries where the gospel was being preached.

I missed all-night prayers in Sharjah. We did well in Sohar. Immigrant workers were longing to be with the Lord the whole night; their longing was to worship the Lord and bring all their wants and needs to the Lord's feet. We praise God. Sometimes it is our needs and wants that bring us to the Lord's feet. If all things went smoothly, we might not look to God in worship. Jesus, please keep me to Yourself. Let there be great love and bondage of the Holy Spirit in us in Trinity. The congregation in Sharjah was a very rich congregation, except for a very few needy ones who waited on the Lord in faith for their needs.

I did have some all-night prayers with Ethiopians. There were ladies and two or three young men who were the musicians. They were excellent worshippers. I was immensely happy that I could be one of them to worship the Lord. Moreover, they met at our house for all-night prayers. You may ask me, not knowing the Ethiopian language, how I would join them in worship and all-night intercession when it was all in their language. *I can only say I moved with the Holy Spirit, which was in them and also in me. Praise God!*

Our Sweet Little Calico Cat, Sweetie!

Our parents picked up a pet dog when my older brother was born. My brother's name was Jaya, and they named the dog as Jerry. We siblings loved Jerry a lot, especially my brother Jaya, who was very fond of Jerry. Jerry was twelve years old when he died, and all of us cried bitterly. Then my parents took another dog, Aron. He also died after six months. All of us cried again. Then my parents decided not to have any pets in the house. That was the end of it. Ernest's mother was also very fond of pets. She would even feed them with spoons. In any case, Ernest and I never wanted a pet in the house.

On summer midafternoons, when the temperature was 104 degrees Fahrenheit, the single huge brown front door of our house was wide open. As we walked toward the door, we noticed a cute white little calico kitten standing near the doorstep. It was drooped down, almost dead in the heat; in any second, she would collapse. Her refined mannerism was such that though the door was wide open, she wouldn't enter the house unless we took her in. We looked at her with our wide-open eyes, and

I passionately said, "She is going to die any second. Let's take her in."

That was the beginning of my sweet, cute calico cat in our lives. The very first day, she worried us by not eating at all. She would cuddle up in a corner of the living room and refuse to eat.

Well, that was the first day. On the second day, she revived. She began to eat and exhibit her skills, which amused us. We had great amusement and fun watching her. She would jump from chair to chair. She would crawl at the bottom edge of the center table! She would get into a plastic bag and roll over to amuse herself! She would never let me read the newspaper. Perhaps she believed that those papers were harmful to me. She would try to jump over it and pull it away from me. Our bedrooms were upstairs. As we climbed up the staircase, she would come running, walk in between our legs, zigzag, and see that we carried her upstairs.

Our love for our calico kitten oozed out of us naturally. It appeared that by all her tricks, she conquered us. Admiring her beauty and love, we called her Sweetie, though we called her in many different names—she responded to all of them. It appeared to us our tone toward her was more familiar to her than the names. Thus, we became a family of three. Our friends in Dubai also encouraged us to keep the cat and not to send her away, for they also had great joy in bringing up their Ginger, which had fallowed them home while they were returning from a walk. They gave all good gifts for our pet.

We never wanted an animal in our bedroom. Having an animal in our bedroom was something that we would never tolerate. So, during the nights, we locked ourselves in. When we woke up in the mornings, we would see her waiting for us near the door. Perhaps she never left the place the whole night. From then on, our bedroom door was wide open to let her come in as and when she wanted.

She had a chair against the window in our bedroom, facing the street. On the chair we laid a soft pillow, on which she would relax, watching the cars and the people passing by on the street. As she watched, she would slowly go to sleep. Let me tell you, she always cleaned herself up with her cute tiny tongue before she went to sleep. The greatest fun was to watch her go in circles while she cleaned her hind legs. In the middle of some nights, she came to our bed. Sometimes she slept by the side of me, always making sure that her head rested on my shoulders. Though often she preferred to sleep clinging to my leg.

Her doctor told us that if we had to keep her inside the house, we should not let her go out freely. If she went outside, we should not get her inside, as there were stray cats outside with all kinds of diseases and those diseases might also contaminate human beings. So, we had to keep her on a leash so that she might not run out and mingle with other cats. Many people told me that cats steal and eat foodstuffs, especially fish and chicken. I found my sweetie never stealing food. She never ate any other food except her cat food, which she was used to. Sweetie spoke to us in many different sounds and communicated what she wanted. She had mastered a particular "Meow" for particular wants. For example, when she was angry with us when she found us searching for her. When we delayed in seeing her. When she was displeased with us. When she wanted our attention. When she grumbled at us. When she was fearful. When she was very angry with whom she thought were her foes!

She could not understand why she did not have a bedroom of herself when we had a bedroom for ourselves. Therefore, she chose another bedroom, went near the door, and called us to open the door for her; if it was not closed, she would climb on the bed and make us cover her with a sheet. If the bedroom was opened, climbing on the bed, she would still call us to cover her with a sheet. In case we did not respond to her calling, she would keep standing there forever, till we responded. In night times, she was not particular to sleep in a bed of hers, but she would sleep on Ernest's office chair, then Ernest had to pick up a short stool available in the room to use his table. I would laugh and say, "It is like the story of the Arab and the camel."

Often, she made us follow her. Sweetie took us where she wanted to go. She led the way and kept turning back to see if we followed her or not. In case we didn't follow her, she got back to the original place and waited patiently till we followed her. Sometimes when she reached the destination, she would see that we stood there while she rolled over on the ground. The next alternate to this was, she took us to the backyard and let us sit on the chair while she sat on the ground, clinging to our feet. In Indian culture, clinging to someone's feet is the most humble and respectable thing to do. Sweetie also made us follow her and stand there, watching her, either eating her food or grass.

Just two days ago, she stood near the patio door for a long time, till I went to spread a towel at the corner of the backyard for her to lie down and have a sunbath. They say dogs are faithful and not the cats. My sweetie was always thankful to us for what we did for her. From nowhere she would come to me, kiss my toes, and go on her way. Just to say a word of thanks. We wanted to mute her because she would cry a lot at mating times. I would say our house is God's house and we should maintain peace. Therefore, I believed in taking her for muting. My friend and I took Sweetie to the animal clinic. All along the way, Ernest would phone me and ask me if that was God's will! His last call was when I was at the doorstep of the clinic. I just had to tell Ernest, "There were eunuchs [Esther 1:10] during biblical times too."

The surgery was done, but the stitches were not okay. They used the thread that was used for the camels. As I brought her home, the stitches came off and the wound was wide open. We took her back again, and now they restitched it and put a funnel around her neck. We kept her in a huge cage; if not, she had a habit of jumping up and down, and we fed her with a serving spoon, through the cage. Just as Ernest's mother would do. The difference was, she fed with a teaspoon and we with a serving spoon. The problem wasn't over there—the wound was infected! Finally, by God's grace, she was healed.

There are many stories that I can tell you to illustrate the bond of love for one another as a family of three. I had lost my beautiful gold chain with a blue square stone in it. I searched for it everywhere and couldn't find it. After three days had passed, while both of us were sitting in the front yard, Sweetie went around on the lawn, and as she walked, she stopped and was sniffing something. I wondered what it was. Must be a dead lizard, I thought, but lo and behold, when I went to see, it was my gold chain! If not for my Sweetie, my chain would have gone deep into the dust, as the sprinkler sprinkled water on the lawn every day.

Another such day, I was sitting on a chair, reading, while Sweetie walked around the lawn on the front yard. A lizard from the tree above fell on my book. I screamed with fear, and my Sweetie came running and saw that I ran behind her into the house! Since then, I concluded that Sweetie was an angel sent to us by my God, my heavenly Father. We have no children, and the Lord knew we needed someone with us, and so He sent our Sweetie to our doorstep and gave us a single, united heart to embrace her as our own. It was also Sweetie who enticed us to herself and conquered our love.

It was unfortunate that somebody robbed her. Maybe they thought it was a bred cat, and so they took her for three days, stole her silver chain and the huge cage in which she was kept. On Thursday evenings, we had a church prayer meeting in the house. That Thursday, Ernest would not eat, one can see tears running down his cheeks, so he went upstairs. As Ernest saw her, through the window from upstairs, slowly walking toward the door, the delight of seeing Sweetie coming toward the door was noticed by all in the fellowship. The compound gate was closed. Not sure how she made it. He came running down the steps and embraced her with a welcome. Praise God she was safe! Thus, the prayer of the Thursday fellowship members was answered in God bringing her right on time when they were all there after the prayer, not disturbing their prayer or worship by coming a little earlier. *What a glorious companionship!*

Sweetie is eleven years old now.

Ernest

Ernest came to know the Lord in Sunday school of the same church where I came to know the Lord. He was ten years old when his Sunday school superintendent, a foreign missionary, asked him if he knew his memory verse. After he narrated the memory verse, she asked him if she would see him in heaven. She had always told her children in the Sunday class how to receive Jesus as their Savior.

On a Sunday morning, her husband, the pastor, came to the church, and after he conducted the service, he made an announcement that his wife had fallen asleep in the Lord and the funeral would take place after the service. His wife, the Sunday school superintendent, had cancer, which nobody knew till the day of the glory of her spirit and eternal bliss. She slowly *swept* into the hands of the Almighty. What a sacrificial life that was! There was no treatment of such sickness in India those days. Her tomb is still in India, in our birth city, Mysore.

Ernest accepted Jesus as his Lord and Savior at his mentor's funeral. Even till today, Ernest talks about her, and says when he goes to glory, the first person he would like to see is his Sunday school teacher, who came to India to work with the Muslims, called Zenana Mission. Is it strange that Ernest was in the land of Muslims to intercede for them? From the day of the funeral of his mentor till today, Ernest has been preaching on being born again.

Ernest had two paternal uncles. Both of them had no children. One worked in Australia all his life. The other one worked in foreign services. His wife also worked in foreign services along with her husband. She was supposed to be the richest lady, owning a lot of properties; her father was an engineer in a palace. Both the uncles had prostate gland problems, and both had fallen asleep in the Lord from prostate cancer. This was a serious issue for us as it was a matter of heredity, and Ernest was the only male heir to inherit it. So, we were alert. As the days and years went by, he did experience the prostate gland bothering him, and to our dismay, we discovered, with the help of the doctors, that Ernest did have the prostate gland issue.

It was benign for quite a few years, but then since he had serious issues, we had to attend to it. With the fear of it turning malignant, we wanted it to be terminated. The doctor disagreed with our decision, but they suggested that they do a surgery of kind of abrasion, where they would just scrape the gland and thin it down. That was called turf.

The doctors in that particular hospital did not agree with the benign slides of another hospital. They tried to do one of their own, and the attempt of that also had a lot of infection, and Ernest had a high fever with rigor. I was all by myself next to him, and I had no experience with such a thing called rigor with high infection. I shivered with fear looking at Ernest jumping up and down with high fever. I called the duty doctor, and he did give an injection on the spot, within five minutes, and Ernest was calm and settled down. We praise God. The Lord is with us even when we walk through the shadows of death.

Since Ernest is very sensitive to medicine and the procedure, we continued to have a lot of struggles. They would fill his bladder with water to measure and check the retention, and they could never measure it since it would all get stuck. It happened once, on a Saturday night, and there was nobody to help us out. There was a duty doctor, but he was busy on the phone. We were waiting for him to attend to Ernest till the middle of the night. The torture of waiting there with the bladder full was something beyond description.

Well, the surgery day came in without much looking forward to. That was a huge hospital with a huge operation theater. I heard more than ten people would be operated at a time. We waited outside anxiously till Ernest came out. Our Lord protected his life. He came out, and they took him straight to the room. The fever never left him. The doctors were not sure why the temperature was on and on. We had to stay back till the fever persisted. I had to watch by the night to see if the drip was going all right. During the day, I was to measure the water output. This went on and on for several days. Ernest never spoke much during those days, not sure what was going on in his mind. We waited in the hospital for several days for the fever to come down. His sisters and their spouses were also with us for some days.

The Lord delivered us, and we came back to Sharjah. We thank God for the good congregation members in the church. They were more than our friends, brothers, and sisters in

Christ. We praise God for them. We kept watching the PSA level, for the broken prostate gland was still intact. We noticed slowly the PSA level increasing. There came a day, once again, that they had to do a biopsy. In the ten slides they took out, one of them showed cancer for 0.5 percent. So, we had to now get it removed. The doctor told us not to worry because the growth of the cancer was very slow. And so as per his age, it would be in his system with no serious issues. We were quite adamant that it be taken out, mainly because of what had happened to his two uncles.

We had only to consult our Jesus regarding this; we studied all about the surgical procedures and came to an understanding that only robotic surgery would be safe for the prostate gland, as it was round in shape and the wrist of the doctor would not take a round around the gland, and therefore, there would be a lot of bleeding. We considered India, and then we were given an understanding that robotic surgery was just a new thing in India; therefore, we did not have the boldness to get it done in India. We were not sure how to get around it; there were issues to be taken care of. As we were thinking and praying about our next move, *the Lord brought an angel to our house.*

She was an American missionary who was then in Sharjah. We shared the problem with her. To our amazement, she said that her husband had the same problem. The doctor who did the surgery for them was excellent, and so on and so forth. She was most willing to give his details. She would also make an arrangement to live with another elderly couple same as our age. After all these talks were over, all three of us prayed and wept, thus sharing the love, joy, and passion of the Lord. That was a very touching time. She left us with the online details of the doctor.

I went on Google and checked the urology doctors. I applied and got connected to the doctor. Meanwhile, our friend who had promised to find a host family for us did find the host family. The couple was a godly couple and loved the Lord and the Lord's children. At the immigration, when we arrived, the immigration asked us the reason we were visiting the US and how many dollars we had with us. Ernest did say that we had 10,000 dollars and he was going to get a prostate gland surgery done. We had been several times to the US by now, and we never had such a serious interview, but this time we did, while Ernest was sick.

They took most of us into another immigration room, where many others were there—maybe they wanted to check how much money all of us had with us. In any case, we had to wait for a long time as we were in a long line. We were slightly worried if we would miss our flight for our destination. By God's help, we were able to make it; it was quite delayed by the time we arrived at our destination. Our host couple was still patiently waiting for us at the entrance. What a great exhibit of God's love! It was a great pleasure to meet them. They were a little older than us. They took us to their house and got us introduced to our bedroom and the restroom, their sunroom, and the dining room and kitchen. What a lovely brotherhood in Christ and the joy of meeting a couple who was different in culture!

Is it strange? We make mistakes, but will the Lord also make mistakes? We had to discuss the doctor to be seen, the date of the appointment, etc. To our surprise, this doctor whom we had to see was a different doctor from the doctor our friend in our house in Sharjah had recommended. To our surprise, this doctor whom we had to meet was the same doctor whom our host was going to. Our host also had prostate cancer! Our friend was highly appreciative of this doctor with whom we had an appointment! He was also a great mission-oriented doctor. He was a strong believer in the Lord Jesus Christ. Praise the Lord! He took a lot of interest in Pastor Ernest.

We had very good health insurance in Dubai. Everything was free. Though we had permission for them to take treatment in the US, the US bill was exorbitant. This particular doctor knew that we would not be able to meet with a huge medical bill, so he made all arrangements to do the surgery on a sponsored basis and asked Ernest also to see them. Well, all worked well. The doctor also found an anesthetist for the surgery. This doctor was also a believer, who agreed to do it for free.

The doctor faced one main problem: since Ernest had the turf of the prostate gland already, he knew that the gland was not round, and so he told Ernest he might have to cut him open for the surgery. So, Ernest had to permit him. We had no option, now that we came to the US mainly for the robotic surgery; we did agree for the open surgery. The doctor also said that the growth of the malignancy was a very slow one, so it would be better to just leave. All these were his loud thinking. His final decision was that Ernest looked young and was healthy, so he said, if he did the surgery, he might live another twenty years and, being a pastor, serve the Lord for another twenty more years. So, he decided to go ahead and carry on with the surgery. Praise God!

On the day of the surgery, our Oman friend (who I have referred to as the king of the mountain) and his wife came to stay with us. They had taken a room at the hotel. We praise God for the lovely bond that we developed in Christ! The surgery was successful. But the doctor, who met us the next day, told us on the day of the surgery he experienced a kind of disturbance in his thought. He did not want to do the surgery, but later on, when his wife got up at four in the morning, they both prayed and sensed the power of the Lord, which came into his being after he and his wife prayed together. And then he picked up the courage to do the surgery. We praise the Lord. The robotic surgery itself was a success; the doctor need not have to open him up.

After the surgery, they checked if the urethra was properly connected and to see it was not connected. It was a testing period. The Lord was with us, though. Every time Ernest went in for the testing, he would come out with eyes filled with tears. It was a sad sight for me to see. It took about four weeks to get connected, and Ernest had to go four times to check it up. Our host and hostess were always cheerful in helping us out in driving to the hospital back and forth. The urethra had just gotten connected when the doctor almost decided to open up Ernest again and fix the problem.

We stayed with our host family for about two months, as Ernest had developed certain other infections on the stomach where the surgery holes were made. We then came to know that Ernest was allergic to iodine. No medicine or ointment could work on it to heal the rashes he had developed. Finally, after we came to Dubai, we met a wound specialist who suggested Vaseline or pure honey could sort out the problem. Once a little bit of Vaseline was applied, the wound got healed. A simple medicine, of course, for a long-persistent red rash. With a swollen stomach. This reminded us about Jesus healing the blind with a spit on the ground.

The best part of our time with our host friends is unforgettable. We praise God every second of those enjoyable times. Our habits, desires, and spiritual inclinations were all synchronized very well. While Ernest was in the hospital, I was there with him day and night. They kept him for a long time there because of his fever, as it was in the previous procedure, where the fever never came down, and also the urethra, which never got connected. Every day our friends visited us and we had lunch or dinner together.

The remaining days that we stayed in their house for two months, we were made for each other a couple of times; there was no difference in color or race and in our attitude to each other. During the mornings, both the ladies would get the breakfast ready, after which we would go to the sunroom and sit for prayer. They had a prayer book for the missionaries, they would read the Bible and the prayer request for the missionaries around, and after sharing the family issues, we would pray together. All of us would pray lengthy prayers to our hearts' content.

They had an issue with their son, who was divorced. He knew the Lord but had gone astray and was dating another lady. They had gone through a lot of hurt in the process of the separation of their son's first marriage. They had three grandchildren, two for their son and one girl for their daughter. They were very fond of their grandchildren. Their daughter was well settled. We were immensely happy to know that their grandson had now turned to the Lord and their grandson was instrumental in winning over the father back to the Lord. Their son also got remarried to the mother of his children. It was the children who got their parents together. We praise God! The prayers we said on their behalf were greatly answered.

After the lengthy prayer that we enjoyed together, men would get back to their work and we ladies would go shopping, buying groceries—what great fun! We came home and cooked for noon. After the lunch, we would relax and rest till four, then get back again at four for a cup of coffee, and normally we would order our dinner from outside. If Ernest was well, we would also go out for dinner, and the bill was always on our side. Since they hosted us, that was our great pleasure.

After the dinner, we would watch every day Bill Gaither's worship songs. They had all the collection of Bill Gaither's songs. Every day we watched a different one. We enjoyed every bit of it. They would be on their recliners, and we would be on our recliners. The hostess would then cut the apples and bring it to us; we would eat it while enjoying our conversations. We prayed together again before we said good night and went to sleep. Since then I would like to have a house as they had, with lots of Bill Gaither's videos. I couldn't find anybody so far who showed keen interest to listen to Bill Gaither's video and enjoy them with us.

Some years after our visit to our friends, our hostess had a stroke. Our host had lots of issues, mainly concerning cancer, but he was okay. It was now his turn to take care of her. She had lost her senses, and it was very difficult for him to take care of her. We always kept in touch with him and prayed with him. She picked her speech, and her memory also got back. She was okay for several months, after which the Lord took her to glory. He found it very difficult to live without her and always wanted to join her in glory. Cancer took over him; he knew he would join her soon. He told us that he got the whole house painted. Perhaps he got it ready for his son. As expected, he fell asleep in the Lord's glory. We praise God! Perhaps we would never get to find such great friendship and shared love in Jesus. We would see them in glory. What a hope!

In Concluding Our Work in Sharjah

God was with us as we moved on to Sharjah to take over the church. God was with us when the burglars came to our bedroom while we were fast asleep. God was with us when we met several car accidents. God saved our lives when we were to die in the running wadi waters. God was with us for our thirty years of missionary work in the Middle East. He kept His promise that He gave in Isaiah 41:10 (KJV), "Fear thou not; for I [am] with thee: be not dismayed; for I [am] thy God: I will strengthen thee; yea, I will help thee; yea, I will uphold thee with the right hand of my righteousness."

The senior members of the church were in charge of all the functions and activities of the church. Every year the church hosted about ten members of the Campus Crusaders, now called the Bridges, who would come and have group discussions with the members of the church, encouraging them to have a meaningful and friendly conversation with Arabs.

The youth with some seniors were sent to Urbana, in the USA. A team was sent to South Arica for a world intercessory prayer conference. The youth, with some seniors, were sent to London for London Bridges, to meet and greet the Arabs who went there during the summertime. The youth always came back to share about the good conversations they had had with the Arabs in sharing the love of Jesus. What a glorious opportunity that was to pass on the burning candle and the baton to the next generation!

We were to retire from Dubai one year earlier, but the congregation kept us back for one more year, saying, "God used only Solomon to build the temple, though David had the passion and the vision." According to them, not all could build temples; only some chosen one could do that. The church building had to be extended to double the size, for about eighty congregations that met in the Anglican campus, St. Martin's Church. As a result of that, a new building was constructed, and Ernest laid the foundation of that building in Sharjah. Ernest and the group of board members meant for construction of the church in Oman, and the church extension in Sharjah had to consider the financing aspect, and further, they looked out for those who had an experience in establishing project goals and positioning themselves for success. That was a great success. We left Sharjah for good after we had a dedication service for the new structure.

Amazingly, the pattern of the hall construction depicts a huge adorable cross behind the altar.

Our Friends

Joshi

Our Joshi was much younger to us, but he was always a great adviser to us. He loved talking to us. In general, he loved his voice. He was a great scholar and a highly intelligent individual. He worked in India as a staff worker for the Union of Intercollegiate Fellowship of India. Since we all belonged to this Union of Intercollegiate Fellowship of India ever since our college days, there was a kind of love and oneness shared among us. We knew one another well. Joshi applied for his master's in Fuller Seminary, the United States, and he had to write an article on "church growth." His article was well appreciated by the department, and he was given admission with a full scholarship. On his vacation while we were in India during the same time, it so happened that Joshi was also there. Joshi came to our house to see us. It was a great time with him, chatting.

We enjoyed our conversation with him; we laughed and listened to him. Well, he talked, talked, and talked, and we listened, listened, and listened. We enjoyed every bit of what he was talking about. Suddenly, he realized that he had to go to the airport and catch his flight to the US. By the time he reached the airport, his flight had already left. Well, that was our Joshi.

Joshi was extremely happy to know that Ernest was going to study at Fuller Seminary. We went year after year during summer, and He would always come to the airport and pick us up with a warm welcome. He was a vegetarian, but he did not know how to cook his vegetarian food; instead, he would go to Denny's to eat omelet and lived on it and coffee. Once we were there in the US, in Pasadena, he would come to our place and have vegetarian food with us. Ernest loved him a lot and would call every night to make him sit next to him and would feed him to his heart's content.

Joshi was now doing his doctoral program. He preferred to pick us up at Fuller and send us back to the apartment where we stayed and would get back in the evenings for dinner. He would always say with great respect that he preferred to give us a door-to-door service. He never believed that we should drive there, because we went to study and should study and not get caught and get a ticket.

We were in a foreign country, pursuing what God wanted us to do, and at such time, God provided a luxury for us in our mobility. What a God we serve! Joshi was free to do this for us till Ernest finished his studies, which he did only during the summer, his master's in intercultural studies, with ninety-four units, and then his PhD. All in all, it was a period of seventeen summers. *What an amazing God we serve! We can never take these things for granted.*

No Eyes but Passion

In one of the Friday church services, when the church was fully packed, Ernest was preaching from the pulpit. A fine gentleman, the financial controller of a well-known international company, arrived quite late for the church service. He was not attentive to what was going on in the church but was looking all around; he must have been observing all those who were in the church. He had brought his housemaid to the church, as she was a Christian, and she was very particular to attend the church. This gentleman and his wife were also Christians, but he did not want to attend the church. The gentleman left her in the church and was about to go out of the church when he heard Ernest from the Pulpit saying, *"You are not here by accident."* This made the gentleman sit back to hear what Ernest was going to say. He heard it all.

The Holy Spirit worked a miracle in him. He believed in the salvation grace of the Lord. Though he did not understand the entire plan of salvation, something triggered in him. He went home disturbed, and then there was another couple in the same town where he lived. They met together that evening, and they explained to him all about the love of Jesus and the blood of Jesus, which cleanses us from all our sins. Behold he was now a believer in Jesus. "If we confess our sins, he is faithful and just to forgive us our sins, and to cleanse us from all unrighteousness" (1 John 1:9 KJV).

The two couples met together the next day again. They had dinner together. The calmness of the sea around them filled their hearts. There was a celebration in heaven, and as per Luke 15:10 (KJV), "Likewise, I say unto you, there is joy in the presence of the angels of God over one sinner that repenteth." All went well. There was happiness all around as the angels celebrated in heaven; there was celebration among us too. He and his family were attending our Thursday prayers also. He had many doubts regarding scripture, but since he was a genius, he could grasp the biblical theology quickly.

After a week or so, in the middle of the night, we had a phone call saying this gentleman had a cerebral hemorrhage and it was quite serious; he was admitted to the hospital. At that part of the night, both of us left for the hospital. The streets were empty, and everywhere there was quietness—the chirping of the birds was not audible too. They were all in their nest, perhaps blessed with deep sleep. Once again, the hospital atmosphere was also quiet. There were not many people around; we hardly saw any, as it was very late in the night, perhaps the beginning of the day, dawn.

It was easy to find out the room in which he was laid. We entered the room and saw his wife huddled on a chair. It was pathetic to see him in the hospital. All tubes all over him. He was unconscious. We saw his hands, the skin of which was all in circles, like ringworms. I had never seen such a thing in my life. All that we could do was pray. We heard he was highly diabetic and he was highly alcoholic.

Prayer was the only solution to all his problems and recovery. His wife was in a desperate condition. God did give him life. He came out of the hospital. He had received the Lord as his Savior. He gave up his drinks but lost his eyes forever. Both his optic nerves were gone. As a result, he lost his job too. They went to the best eye surgeons, but none could help him.

I understood his problem, as I had some siblings in our school in Oman who had no optic nerves and the doctor could not do anything about it.

Poverty began to strike them. Though his wife was working still, the money was not enough with two children on hand and their education to be taken care of. We constantly prayed for them, and we also prayed a lot for them in the ladies' fellowship. This lady came to our house one day with some homemade sweets. We had a good conversation. She expressed all the problems they had. We prayed together. Ernest was not at home, and I had no money to give her.

We in the ladies' fellowship felt that we should go to their house and pray for them. So, we went and started singing, worshipping the Lord, and praying for them. I am not sure why the tears of my Jesus came to my eyes and I started crying very badly; I cried loudly and prayed. I walked up and down and prayed. The agony for them in me, I cannot explain. Under normal sorrowful situations, I would not normally cry. I felt very shy about it later. But nobody spoke about it later. That was the end of the struggles and sorrows that they underwent; the Lord remarkably blessed them and lifted them. He was stammering, so his wife started witnessing for him. The lady gave testimonies on his behalf. She was just his mouthpiece. I told him that we needed to hear from him.

Being blind, he completed a master's in divinity and then went on to do a PhD, writing many interesting books. His wife helped him in typing and looked after him as her husband and babe. Now he speaks all over and is a very popular personality.

We praise God for his life. And for his wife, for her love and devotion to him.

Dr. Joshi, our friend, visited us in Dubai from the US during the summertime. That was when he met the reverend Dr. Dev Prasad. Both got very friendly and started to communicate, even after Joshi left for the US. They would exchange the conversation with spontaneous poems; one such example is as below. For them, I was the mediator in their conversation; both would pass on their replies in poems and post e-mails on my ID too. Below is the spontaneous conversation of their poems. These were my 2010 mails.

Drums of Destiny

By Dr. Cruz Dev Prasad

Son, we heard your cry and felt your tears
It is hard on us to see your heart in sears
Indeed, your affection, precious and so rare
So was ours we couldn't share
Son, far though we are yet so very near
Lots ahead, cheer up and speed up on high gear
Friends pray, God's near, have no fears
Dazzling successes await in coming years
Son, we heard your cry and felt your tears
Drums of your destiny reverberate smiles and cheers

December 14, 2010

Drums of Death

By Dr. L. R. Joshi

Sager where my parents are buried—
Beside them one day I hope to stand;
as their loss now buried in my heart,
this dance of death is tranquilizin' me.
The stones that marked their deaths—
just scripted my eventual death;
not having my parents is killing me:
There isn't a balm that can soothe me.
The waves of the ocean drownin' me—
and the sands of destiny burying me;
already dried up are those teary eyes,
yet soothin' are these drums of death.

December 14, 2010

Two great on-the-spot, spontaneous poems. Wonder what God would be sharing about these poems in heaven with His inmates. We are the apple of His eyes. He rejoices over us.

Our great friend Joshi succumbed to serious cancer and fell asleep in the Lord. We have no more Joshi and his ever-standing advice. Not sure how he got into serious cancer. There was no hereditary history; neither was he a nonvegetarian. Thus, he had written the poem below:

Dust

By L. R. Joshi

It doesn't matter where you live—
Once you are dead, you're dead.
It doesn't matter how long you live—
Once the beat delays, you're gone.
It doesn't matter how rich you are—
When you die, you're like a pauper.
It doesn't matter how great you are—
By all count, aren't you mere dust?

December 8, 2010

There was another great businessman in the same town. He was the senior most person in the church from Pakistan. He was friendly with all the Anglican bishops down the line. His wife was the one who always handled the Bible study for us. They had no children. They had been in Sharjah for more than forty years as teachers of English. He started an upholstery business, and he was very successful in that. Made a lot of money. He was quite elderly. He was always sick in the hospital because his blood sugar was very high. Whenever he was in the hospital, we would visit him and pray with him and his wife.

One evening, I was at home alone. Ernest had gone to church. This gentleman called me and was full of words. He had never spoken to me more than a sentence, but that evening, he went on and on. He was full of praises for our work in the church. He told me that there were a lot of changes in the church after we went there and the children behaved well and their mannerism was excellent. He went on to say how the children came to him and greeted him, all because of what we taught them in the Sunday school. I am not sure if this kind of good behavior would be because of the Sunday school or because of the parents. It could be mainly because of the parents and they could be growing spiritually in their families.

In any case, he went on and on. I had only to say yes to everything he said. The call went on for about forty minutes. Somehow, it ended, and the next morning, at five o'clock, we had a phone call from the church: the gentleman was no more on earth and had fallen asleep in the Lord, had gone to glory. We heard from his wife that throughout the night, he was periodically saying "Amen." I wonder what he saw, what he heard; the Lord must have been talking to him.

Dr. Cruz Dev Prasad wrote to us a lovely letter:

Dear Pastor Ernest and Sister Lalitha,

As I stumbled on slowly, step by step, amid thundering applause from a strong 1,200-plus audience (I'll e-mail you the photos when I receive them) who had gathered at the GBS (Gilgal Bible Seminary) main hall, my heart was thanking you, Pastor, for it is you who must take the credit for making this happen. And I thank Jesus for blessing me with both of you in my life and the nostalgic, fond, and memorable five years that we were fortunate to spend with you here in St. Martin's. If I say that we miss you, it would be an absolute understatement. Thank you once again, and may God bless both of you for this and all that you have done for me and my family.

Incidentally, I am inclined to use this opportunity to bring to you the fact that as we approach the year's end, the total tally of the churches I have visited to share the "power of the gospel" would be more than 120, including the revisits. And I sincerely thank you for this also because it was the passion and intensity of your sermons that produced a down-to-earth but very compelling and persuasive evangelist in me, which would not have been possible at all without me hearing you at St. Martin's—that fond memory of you behind the pulpit never leaves me and haunts me tearfully while your powerful but incredibly hushed voice reverberates inside my head every time I sit in St. Martin's.

Pastor, every single day I am praying for both of you seven times seven for the Almighty to continue to bless both of you with the best of His best and for Jesus to walk you through your ministry and all your spiritual endeavors powerfully and successfully.

In His Service, Yours Humbly,
Cruz Dev Prasad

He wrote a poem to me too:

Pearl of Pearls
By Cruz Dev Prasad

"She is clothed with strength and dignity,
and she can laugh at the days to come" (Prov. 31:25).
When we thank God for our pastor, we must give Him thanks for two,
For when Pastor came to us, God also blessed us with you.
No matter the hour, whatever the need, you go the extra mile,
Always ready to share a comforting thought and a smile.
May each day bring forth a treasured memory of the past,
And a blessing to make your future dazzle with success so vast.
May all the beauty of God's nature fill your heart with joy and happiness;
May your path always be strewn with His compassion and lovely tenderness.
We love you, are thankful for you, and pray for you daily;
May God bless you as you serve Him richly and joyfully.

Some Reflections

John (1:11 KJV) He came to his own and his own received him not.

1. We believe we are the sons and daughters; we are the adopted children of our Lord. Therefore Christians, Muslims and Jews are the off-spring of Abraham. It was shocking and overwhelming when we asked our Jewish guide on our visit to Israel what he thought of Jesus. He said He was an ordinary man; those days, ordinary men did the miracles, and so did Jesus. Whereas if asked a Muslim friend what they thought of Jesus, they would say, "He was a great prophet." Every Muslim would say the same. Is it too difficult for them to believe in the sacrificial blood of Jesus? It is only the names of the religion that build a gulf in between. (Lalitha Victor)
2. More often than not, plentiful harvests are not visible to the human eye but through the eyes of faith. Over the years, it becomes visible, so never despair. (Dr. Ernest Victor)
3. Zwemer would want the remembrance of the one hundredth anniversary of his birth to do just two things: first, to point others to Christ, whom he loved and served with such fidelity, and second, to inspire the churches to greater effort to reach the world of Islam with the gospel and to win young people to consecrate their lives to that most difficult type of mission service. Being dead, our brothers will speak. (Samuel Zwemer, New York, April 12, 1867)

4. "Let me burn out for God." (First modern apostle to Islam, Henry Martin)
5. "But when he saw the multitudes, he was moved with compassion on them, because they fainted, and were scattered abroad, as sheep having no shepherd. Then saith he unto his disciples, the harvest truly is plenteous, but the laborers are few" (Matt. 9:36–37 KJV). (Ernest Victor)
6. Those who follow Christ are called Christians, but Jesus came to earth not for Christians alone but for the entire world. "For God so loved the world that he gave his only begotten Son, that whosoever believeth in him should not perish, but have everlasting life" (John 3:16 KJV). Perhaps calling ourselves Christians is not a good idea! But how do we identify ourselves with Christ? Our very life will have to reflect the love of Jesus. (Lalitha Victor)
7. There will come a day, please, God, when Arabs from ——will travel in their sailboats much farther than Socotra, not to find pearls, but to catch men. (Dr. Paul Harrison, M World 19, p. 73)
8. His Word does not return to Him void; it needs to be complemented by living witness. A consecrated life is a living epistle, not in a dumb resignation. (Van Perusem, "Village Evangelism in Oman," M. World, 1920–1921)

We lift our hands on high.
Not like the nerveless fatalists.
Content trust and die.
Our faith springs like the eagle.

That soars to meet the sun.
And cries exulting unto thee.
O! Lord Thy will be done!
—"The Moslem World," by Samuel M Zwemer

Thy kingdom come. Thy will be done.
Throughout the Muslim world.

For thine is the kingdom, the power,
and the glory, forever and ever. Amen.

Epilogue

My life journey can be summarized in saying "the Lord has done great things for us and we are filled with joy....Those who go out weeping, carrying seed to sow, will return with songs of joy, carrying sheaves with them" (Ps. 126:3, 5 NIV).

As I ponder on my life journey, there is indeed a Spirit sense that by His grace and for His glory, I am finishing well. There is an inner confidence that I will hear the Master say, "Well done good and faithful servant...enter into the joy of the Lord" (Matt. 25:21 KJV).

I leave behind this legacy with much hope and prayer that some young lives will take on this challenge and live a full life for Jesus Christ, our Lord and God.

As I advance in age and intimacy with Jesus, I am confident that the Lord has led me to write this book for His glory and for the encouragement of the missionaries who would venture into the mission field after us. Amen.

Love so amazing, so divine. Demands my soul, my life, my all...

About the Author

Lalitha Victor is the founder of two schools, one in South India and the other in the Sultanate of Oman. A teacher educator and an assistant professor of education for thirteen years, she served with the Ministry of Education in India and Oman for thirty-two years. She is the author of the Pearl Sunday school curriculum and trained some youth of Oman to passionately teach the kids. A teacher of Sunday schools since the age of sixteen, Lalitha directed vacation Bible school for five years.

CPSIA information can be obtained
at www.ICGtesting.com
Printed in the USA
FSHW020821250221
78888FS